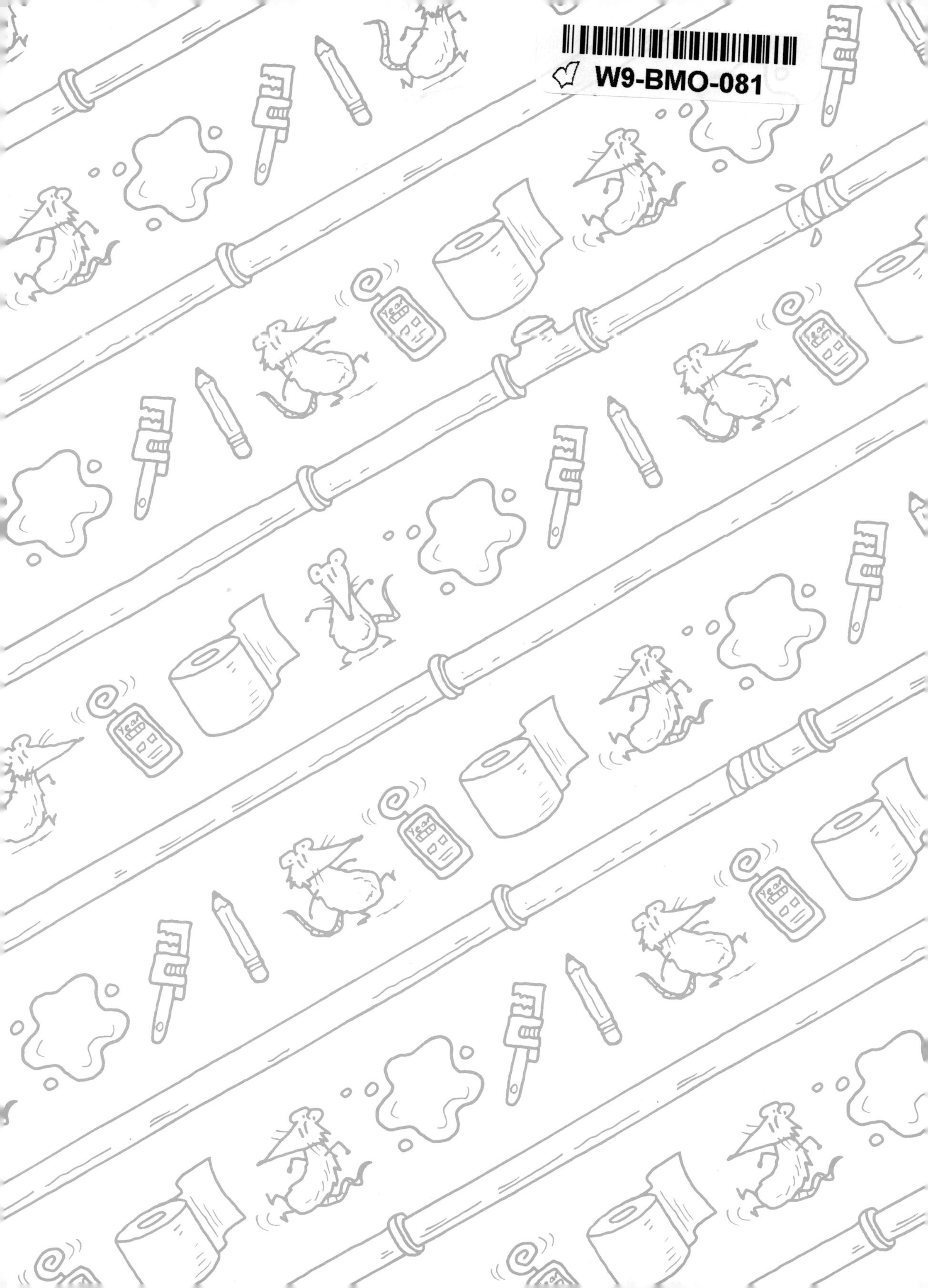

W9-BMO-081

Uncle John's iFlush Plunging into Mystery

BATHROOM READER FOR KIDS ONLY!

by
Patrick
Merrell

No Limburger past this point

Bathroom Readers' Press
Ashland, Oregon

UNCLE JOHN'S IFLUSH: PLUNGING INTO MYSTERY
BATHROOM READER® FOR KIDS ONLY

Copyright © 2014 by the Bathroom Readers' Press
(a division of Portable Press). All rights reserved. No part of
this book may be used or reproduced in any manner whatsoever
without written permission, except in the case of brief
quotations embodied in critical articles or reviews.

"Bathroom Reader," "Bathroom Readers' Institute," and "Portable Press"
are registered trademarks of Baker & Taylor. All rights reserved.

For information, write:
The Bathroom Readers' Institute
P.O. Box 1117
Ashland, OR 97520
www.bathroomreader.com

Book design and illustration by Patrick Merrell, www.patrickmerrell.com

ISBN-10: 1-62686-042-4 / ISBN-13: 978-1-62686-042-1

Library of Congress Cataloging-in-Publication Data
Uncle John's iFlush plunging into mystery bathroom reader for kids only!
pages cm
Summary: "Trivia, quotes, history, etc. in the typical Uncle John's
format"—Provided by publisher.
ISBN 978-1-62686-042-1 (hardback)
1. Wit and humor, Juvenile. 2. Curiosities and wonders--Juvenile
literature. I. Bathroom Readers' Institute (Ashland, Or.)
II. Title: iFlush plunging into mystery bathroom reader for kids only.
PN6166.U5355 2014
081—dc23
2014004552

Printed in the United States of America
First Printing: May, 2014

18 17 16 15 14 6 5 4 3 2 1

Thanks! A hearty high-four (sorry, that's all the fingers I have) to some humans who helped make this book possible:

Gordon Javna, Jay Newman, Blake Mitchum, Erin Corbin, Kim T. Griswell, Trina Janssen, Hannah Halliday, Brandon Walker, Brian Boone, Aaron Guzman, Joan Kyzer, Thomas Crapper

Portable Press and iFlush are not affiliated with or endorsed by Axent or iFlush tankless
toilets in any way. For more information about Axent visit www.axentinternational.ch.

iOpener

Greetings

The Four P's invisible neighbor, Ms. Tinnius, is in the house…er, lab! Since she knows a thing or two about unusual happenings (read more about her on page 49), I asked her to help me plan out the mysterious journey you're about to take.

What's in store…er, lab? Glad I asked! Here's just a glimpse:

- **Germany:** Clever Hans, the Four-legged Adding Machine
- **The Atlantic Ocean:** *Mary Celeste*, Ghost Ship
- **16th-Century Europe:** Strasbourg's Dancing Plague
- **Ancient Egyptians:** Do You Eat Crocodiles in Your Dreams?
- **The White House:** Beware the Secret Service Defenses
- **Middle Ages:** The Pea-headed Children of Woolpit, plus
- **An Undersea Voyage in the iFlush Sub!**

Whenever you're ready, go to the…

Intro on page 6

and we're off and flushing!

Contents

PAGE	YEAR	ARTICLE	iPUZZLE
6	Now	Bathrooom User…	Introduction
8	1610	Gobbledybook	Reprint
10	1968	Cosmo Not	Space Race
12	1952	Monsters! Eek!	Monster Hunt ▶
14	1972	Inside Man	Wat•erg•ate
16	1512	Witch Way	Which Witch? ▶
18	1872	Ghost Ship	Sea-doku
20	1960	Out There	The Drake Equation
22	1888	It's a Secret!	Label Maker ▶
24	1982	Tweet Free	Bird Watching
26	2014	Do Not Enter!	The Prez
28	1795	The Money Pit	The Rock
30	1999	Don't Look at This Page	Paradox ▶
32	1518	Crazy Legs	May I Cut In?
34	1672	Wild Child	Tarzan of the Apes
36	1958	Bombs Away	Missing Bomb
38	1828	Lava Land	Canoe Find It?
40	1997	The Bloop	Oops! ▶
42	1916	Sixth Sense	Mind Reader
44	1225 B.C.	Dream On	Good or Bad?
46	1990	Clipped Art	Concert-tration
48	Now	Bathroom Break	Ms. Tirrius

PAGE	YEAR	ARTICLE	iPUZZLE
50	1896	High Lights	Look! Up in the Sky!
52	1996	Baigong Pipes	Pipe Up ▸
54	1990	Hidden Meaning	Spy Jokes
56	1952	Super Sleuths	Whodunit?
58	70 B.C.	Island Time	Like Clockwork ▾
60	1198	Human Beans	Greenery
62	1914	Puzzle King	How Puzzling
64	950 B.C.	"What's the Password?"	Rat Latin
66	1904	Horse Sense	Whinny Ha-Ha
68	1937	Stones in the Sticks	Stone Work ▸
70	1812	Waves Goodbye	Something's Different
72	1941	It's a "Dirty" Job	What's Dot?
74	1885	Buried Treasure	Buried Letters
76	2014	Didya Ever Wonder?	Whadya Think? ▸
78	1782	Toad-ally Awesome	Hop to It
80	1947	What Was That?	UFOdoku ▸
82	2012	Mystery Moolah	List Price
84	2014	Sub Way	Seascape Escape
86	1925	"Z" End	Fawcett Search
88	Now	The End	Ridiculous Quiz
90	Now	Answers	
96	Now	Create a Mystery Hunt	Activity

Bathroom user...

... prepare to dive into the greatest **toilet-themed adventure** ever devised by a group of **mad-scientist-type plumbers** and hosted by a bedraggled-yet-charming **lab rat** named **Dwayne**. That's me.

But, first, a quick explanation.

Copying how **computers** have been connected together to form the **Internet**, a top-secret plumbing team known as the **Four P's** linked the world's **sewer lines** together to create the **Interpipe**. You probably think I'm making that up, but this book is based on how it actually works!

Flush yourself down a toilet in **Walla Walla** (that's a city in the northwest part of the United States), and next thing you know you're in **Katmandu** (that's like all the way on the other side of the world).

Wait, it gets even better!

The Four P's also created a waterproof device called the **iSwirl** that can be used to travel back in time, spinning through the years in a mere flush of the toilet! Is that not totally cool... and wet?

Yeah, I thought you'd agree.

So here's how this is going to work.

I'm gonna flush myself down this toilet, and you're gonna follow along. I'll be visiting a **different place** and a **different year** every time you turn the page. Solve the **puzzle** you find there, and you can move on— in one of three ways.

1. Follow the **pipes** to the next page; **2.** jump to the page shown on the **iSwirl** (in the lower right-hand corner) to travel through the book in order from the earliest date to the most recent; or **3.** visit pages any old way you want!

Sound like a plan?

Then let's get going! I'll jump in, you turn the page, and away we GO!

Note:

If you want to keep your book clean, use a separate piece of paper (toilet paper not recommended!) for solving the puzzles.

Go to the page shown.

1610

Where: The north wing of Prague Castle, home to Emperor Rudolph II's art collection, including a…

Gobbledybook

A section of one page in the book

I call it that because the book is filled with strange writing and drawings of unknown plants and other weird things. The moment **Rudolph II** saw it, he had to have it, believing it to be the work of the great 13th-century philosopher **Roger Bacon**. The price: 600 gold ducats (about $90,000 today).

Rudolph was an art nut. He spent a lot more time buying it than he did ruling the countries under his control—**Germany**, **Austria**, **Hungary**, and a couple of others. Inside his castle walls, he assembled Europe's largest collection of paintings, sculptures, mechanical devices, fancy swords, and other decorative doodads.

In spite of his fascination with the book, Rudolph could never make any sense of its nearly 300 pages. Neither could his brainy mathematicians and scientists. It's written in some kind of code, using an unknown language.

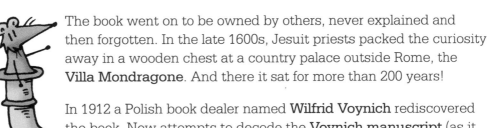

The book went on to be owned by others, never explained and then forgotten. In the late 1600s, Jesuit priests packed the curiosity away in a wooden chest at a country palace outside Rome, the **Villa Mondragone**. And there it sat for more than 200 years!

In 1912 a Polish book dealer named **Wilfrid Voynich** rediscovered the book. New attempts to decode the **Voynich manuscript** (as it came to be known) began. But nobody could crack its secrets. Not World War I and II code breakers. Not even modern-day computers.

Some suggested it couldn't be read because it's nothing more than impressive-looking nonsense. But nobody has proved that, and many doubt it. Most experts think it too closely resembles real language to be a meaningless, random creation. The *only* thing that is certain after all these years—it's one very weird book.

The *Voynich* manuscript is about the size of this book, except four times as thick.

Prague Castle is the largest antique castle in the world.

iPuzzle

Reprint

Find 10 differences between the original page on the left and the altered one on the right (there are no changes to individual words).

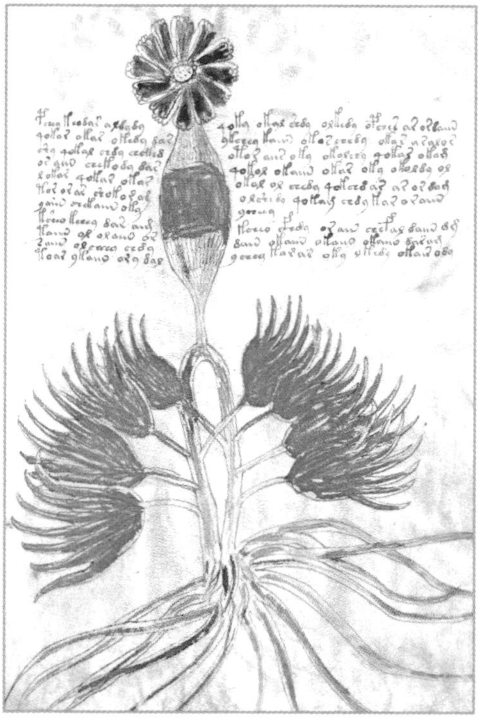

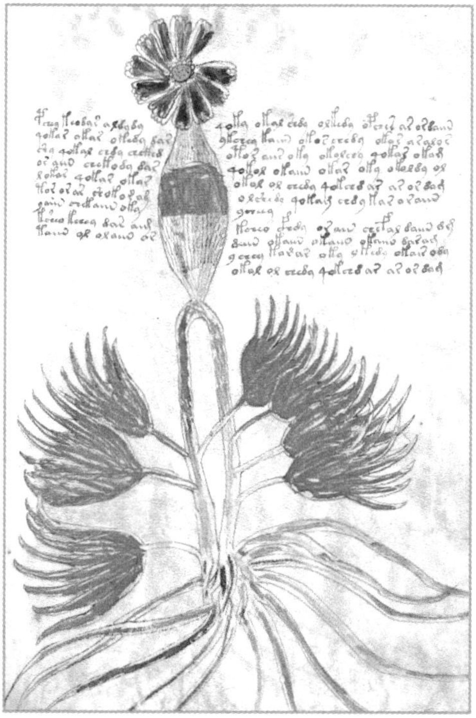

Why couldn't the two books get along?
They weren't on the same page.

Testing, Testing: In 2009 University of Arizona scientists dated paper samples from the Voynich manuscript by analyzing the carbon in them. Their conclusion—the paper was made between 1404 and 1438. The McCrone Institute of Chicago dated the ink to about the same time.

Jump to this page **or** follow the pipes.

Some experts think the Voynich manuscript's text is about medicine.

1968 **Where:** The Chkalovsky airbase near Moscow, Russia, scene of cosmonaut Yuri Gagarin's last flight

RIA Novosti

Gagarin in space, 1961: "It's Actually Happened!"

Cosmo Not

Less than seven years ago, **Yuri Gagarin** soared to worldwide fame as the first man in space. Overnight, he became the Soviet Union's biggest hero.

So it was a huge shock today, March 27, when Gagarin, age 34, crashed and died during a flight in a **MiG-15** trainer jet. His instructor, Colonel Vladimir Seryogin, sitting behind him, died as well.

Investigators wrote up a 29-volume report. But **Soviet president Leonid Brezhnev** felt releasing it in full would "unsettle" an already saddened nation. A brief public statement explained that weather balloons, masked by cloudy skies, had caused Gagarin to swerve into a deadly spin.

A lot of people didn't buy that. They wondered what really happened, and rumors began to swirl.

Was an air vent left open in the cockpit, causing Gagarin to black out? Had he been distracted while taking pictures of birds? Or shooting deer? Was he drunk? Did aliens capture him? Was it a plot by President Brezhnev, jealous of the cosmonaut's fame? Why hadn't he or his instructor ejected? Some even suggested Gagarin's death had been faked.

The questions and wild theories continued for another 45 years. Finally, in 2013, officials revealed the truth. Another pilot in a supersonic **Su-15** jet had flown too close to Gagarin. The "backwash" of air flipped the smaller MiG-15, forcing it into a deep spiral. Gagarin never stood a chance.

Just one secret remains—the identity of the other pilot. Officials acknowledged it was a former cosmonaut, alive and in his 80's, but felt sharing his name "will fix nothing."

By 2010, over 500 people had gone into space.

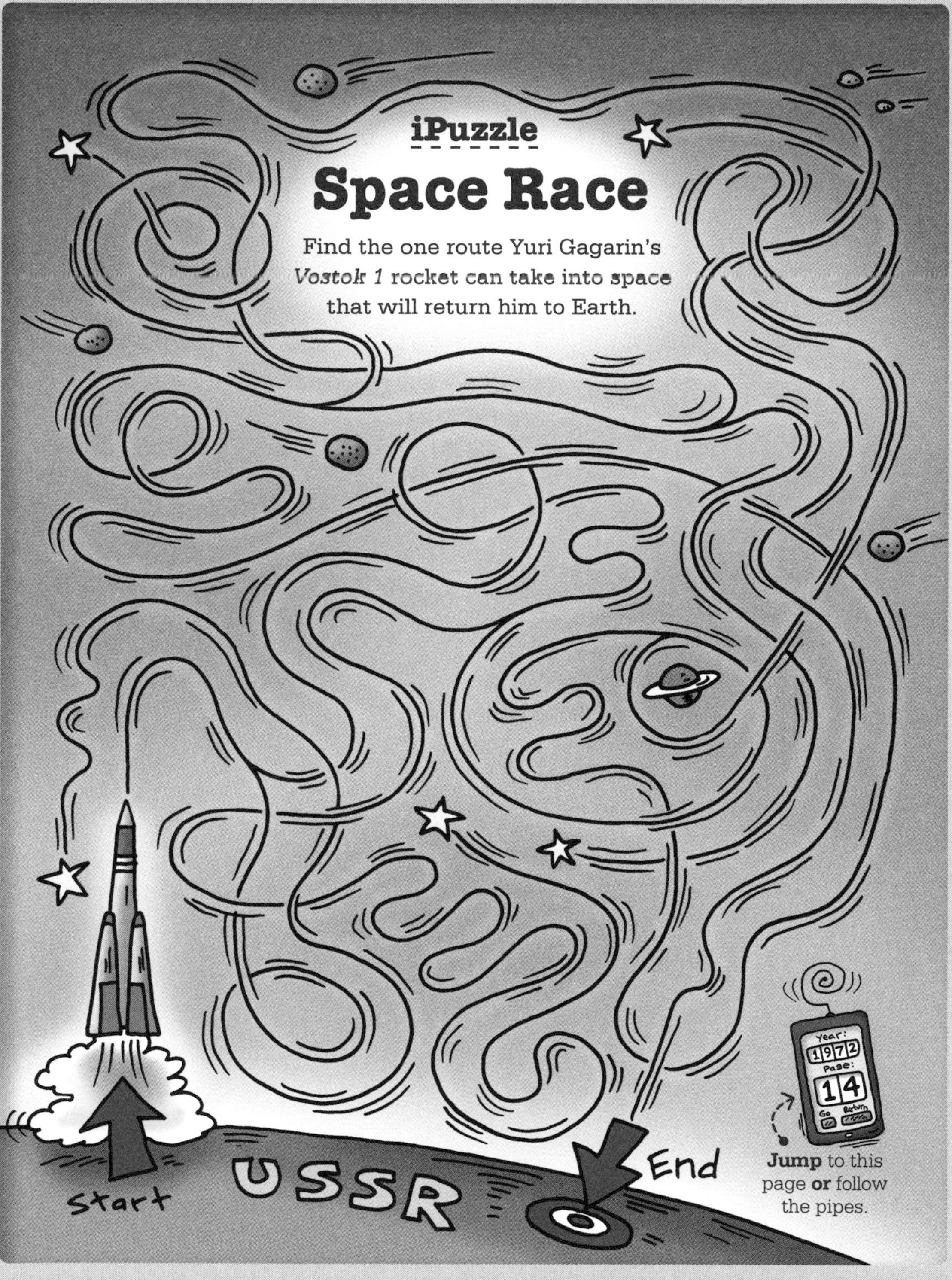

Spending a month in space can add two inches to your height (lack of gravity stretches out the spine).

1952

Where: Around the world looking for creatures that go bump in the night...and day

Monsters! Eek!

People are always seeing monsters. Or thinking they have. Here's my top-four list of monsters...that didn't turn out to be.

The Phantom of Flatwoods: In 1952 residents of **Flatwoods, West Virginia**, reported seeing a glowing-red spaceship crash-land. Soon after, a man-sized creature with an ace-of-spades-shaped head and clawed fingers hissed and flew at a group of boys. In 2000 the **Committee for Skeptical Inquiry** suggested it was nothing more than a meteor and a large barn owl.

Chupacabra: In 1995 people in **Puerto Rico** started finding dead farm animals, their blood drained as if by a vampire. The culprits: ghostly blue-skinned creatures dubbed chupacabras ("goatsuckers" in Spanish). Sightings of similar evil red-eyed beasts followed in Mexico, Texas, South America, and even Asia. Fifteen years later scientists concluded the chupacabras were merely **coyotes** and **wild dogs** suffering from **mange**, a disease that left them scrawny and hairless.

Hogzilla: In 2004 a hunting guide named **Chris Griffin** claimed he'd shot a gigantic wild hog in the swamps of **Georgia**—12 feet long and 1,000 pounds (3.7 m, 450 kg)! That turned out to be true... sort of. **National Geographic** pig specialists dug up the porker's body, measuring it at 7.5 feet and 800 pounds. Enormous, sure, but a DNA test identified it as half domestic pig, suggesting it might have been raised and fattened on a farm.

Bigfoot: Bigfoot sightings stretch back centuries, many of them hoaxes. In 2008 two men announced they'd found the corpse of a huge hairy manlike creature by a creek in **Georgia**. Closer inspection revealed that one of its big feet was rubber. Also, its fur burned into a melted ball, something real hair doesn't do.

Puerto Rican comedian Silverio Pérez claims to have invented the name *Chupacabra*.

Two other names for Bigfoot: Sasquatch and Skookum.

iPuzzle

Monster Hunt

Find each monster on the list by circling it in the grid.
Look for words reading forward, backward, up, down, or diagonally.

BEAST
BIGFOOT
BLOB
BRUTE
CHUPACABRA
CREATURE
CYCLOPS
DEMON
FIEND
GIANT
HOGZILLA
MUMMY
OGRE
PHANTOM
VAMPIRE
WEREWOLF
ZOMBIE

N	T	S	A	E	B	X	Z	O	U	C	S
O	E	B	L	S	M	O	T	N	A	H	P
M	T	F	L	O	W	E	R	E	W	W	O
E	U	O	I	O	I	J	Q	R	L	A	L
D	R	K	Z	V	B	M	V	I	Q	Q	C
N	B	I	G	F	O	O	T	P	T	R	Y
E	R	G	O	T	J	C	A	M	E	G	C
I	I	C	H	U	P	A	C	A	B	R	A
F	E	G	G	I	A	N	T	V	I	L	I
U	T	F	Y	M	M	U	M	V	A	U	P
W	E	O	I	M	R	F	S	U	Q	R	K
D	L	W	V	E	I	B	M	O	Z	N	I

Why won't anyone kiss Dracula?
He has bat breath.
What's the best thing to say to a monster with two heads?
Bye bye!
Billy Bob
Year: 1958
Page: 36
Go
Return

Jump to this page **or** follow the pipes.

The Gila monster, a poisonous lizard, is the only real creature with the word "monster" in its name.

1972

Where: Parking space D32 in a deserted garage beneath an office building in Arlington, Virginia—at 2:00 in the morning!

D-Level Inside Man

Deep Throat got his nickname because all his information was on "deep background" (not directly quoted).
32

I'm here to listen in on a secret meeting between *Washington Post* reporter **Bob Woodward** and an informer nicknamed **Deep Throat**. Why are they here?

In June 1972, **President Nixon**'s re-election committee hired five men to break into the opposition's headquarters at the **Watergate complex**. They wanted information. But a security guard caught the burglars, two of whom had address books connecting them to the **White House**. Yikes!

Nixon himself stated that "no one in this Administration, presently employed, was involved in this very bizarre incident." But Deep Throat helped **Woodward** discover that wasn't true.

For more than a year, Deep Throat provided inside information that guided Woodward and his reporting partner, **Carl Bernstein**, in their investigation. One by one, top Nixon officials fell. And on August 8, 1974, Nixon was forced to resign after recordings exposed his attempts to cover up the scandal.

Nixon

Who was Deep Throat? People started asking that question the moment Woodward and Bernstein first mentioned the shadowy figure in their 1974 book, ***All the President's Men***.

News articles suggested many possibilities—Nixon aides, White House lawyers, CIA and FBI officials, and Secret Service technicians who had access to tapes of Oval Office conversations (Nixon's presidential office).

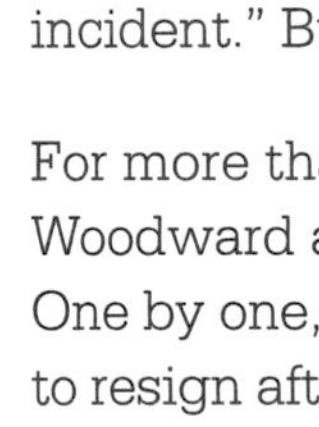
Deep Throat

But, for 33 years, Woodward kept the promise he'd made to Deep Throat from the start. He would not reveal his identity. At least, not until after his informers death. In the end, Deep Throat outed himself. On May 31, 2005, at age 91, ***Vanity Fair*** magazine published his admission—**Mark Felt**, the No. 2 official at the **FBI**, was Deep Throat.

. . . In 1972 Nixon appointed a loyal man, L. Patrick Gray, as head of the FBI, passing over Mark Felt.

. . . The FBI, the *U.S.*'s top crime-investigating agency, has the fingerprints of more than 90 million pe

iPuzzle

Wat•erg•ate

Each word below can be completed by filling the three blanks with either the first three letters (in order) of Watergate (W-A-T), the second three (E-R-G), or last three (A-T-E).

1. N E W S C A S T
2. __ A __ P L U __
3. __ __ I S __
4. P __ N __ H __ R
5. I C __ B E __ __
6. __ F __ __ R
7. M __ T __ R __ S S
8. __ N E __ __ Y
9. S __ E __ __ Y
10. C __ S __ L __

Time yourself on the first column of 10 answers.
Then see if you can beat it for the second column.
TICK
TICK
60

11. A V __ __ A __ E
12. B R E __ __ H __
13. S T __ R __ L __
14. __ __ L L E __
15. __ R E __ __ H
16. R O __ B O __ __
17. U N D __ __ D O __
18. C H __ P __ __ R
19. __ M E __ __ E
20. C __ N __ E __ N

EXTRA CREDIT

Each pair of answers, combined, is an anagram of WATERGATE (all the same letters, rearranged). Use the clues to figure out each pair.

1. Excited to go: ___ ___ ___ ___ ___

   Light bulb unit: ___ ___ ___ ___

2. Halloween goody: ___ ___ ___ ___ ___

   Hourly pay: ___ ___ ___ ___

3. Archery need: ___ ___ ___ ___ ___ ___

   Amazement: ___ ___ ___

Jump to this page **or** follow the pipes.

In 1976, the movie *All the President's Men* (about the Watergate scandal) won four Academy Awards.

1512 **Where:** In a cave in Knaresborough, England, birthplace of Mother Shipton, a woman who could predict the future

Witch Way

19th-century booklet →

Was **Mother Shipton** real or just a local myth? Nobody's sure. The story goes that a girl named **Ursula Sontheil** was born here in 1488. She later came to be known as Mother Shipton after marrying a local carpenter, Toby Shipton.

Eighty years after Mother Shipton's death, in 1641, a Londoner named **Richard Lownds** first printed her story. It included her most famous prediction, that **Cardinal Wolsey** would see the city of **York**, but never reach it. Enraged when he heard that, Wolsey set out for York. He did view the city from a castle tower eight miles away. But the king called him to **London**, and he died along the way, never reaching York.

In 1862 **Charles Hindley** published a new book that included an astounding poem written by Mother Shipton. Here are a few lines from it:

Carriages without horses shall go,
And accidents fill the world with woe.

Around the world thoughts shall fly
In the twinkling of an eye.

Under water men shall walk,
Shall ride, shall sleep, shall talk.

In the air men shall be seen,
In white, in black, in green.

The world to an end shall come,
In eighteen hundred and eighty-one.

Did Mother Shipton really predict all these things? No, Hindley admitted nine years later. He'd invented the poem to help sales of his book! Such is the legend of Mother Shipton—forever trying to separate fact from fiction.

...Mother Shipton's Cave and a nearby Petrifying Well have attracted tourists for more than 300 years.

Mrs. Salmon's 19th-century London wax museum featured a statue of Mother Shipton. →

iPuzzle

Which Witch?

Below is a woodcut of Mother Shipton from a 1663 pamphlet (color added). Which one is exactly the same as the original?

original

1.

2.

3.

4.

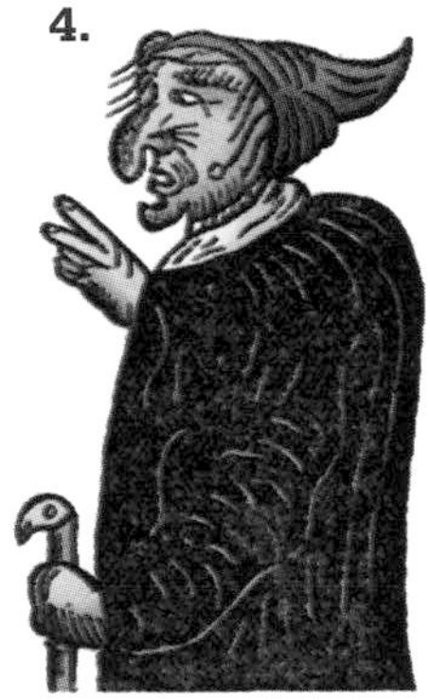

5.

6.

7.

Flying Witch: The Mother Shipton moth, native to Europe and Asia, was given that name because the patterns on its forewings resemble Mother Shipton's profile.

Jump to this page **or** follow the pipes.

A 1903 ad for an Oldsmobile car featured Mother Shipton in it.

→ One of its legs could be swung to kick any child who got too close.

1872 **Where:** Pier 50 in Manhattan aboard the *Mary Celeste*, a ship setting sail for Italy

Ghost Ship

Mary Celeste

One month after the ***Mary Celeste*** left port, another ship, the ***Dei Gratia***, caught sight of it bobbing aimlessly in the water 600 miles (965 km) off **Portugal**. A few lonely sails hung from its masts, one fluttering in shreds.

The captain called out to the ship. He heard...nothing. The first and second mate rowed over to the *Mary Celeste*, then climbed aboard. They found...no one. The ship's wheel rocked back and forth with the waves.

The two men went below. They found neat cabins and the crew's storage chests still filled with their belongings. The ship's cargo, 1,700 barrels of alcohol, remained intact. Aside from a few missing instruments and a jumble of pots and pans on the kitchen floor, everything looked normal.

Shuffleboard anyone?
Anyone?
Hello?

The first mate leafed through the ship's **log**. The last entry had been written 10 days earlier, with no mention of any problems. The *Mary Celeste* had been making good time—then nothing! Had a lifeboat been launched? They couldn't figure out if the ship had even had one.

The eight-man *Dei Gratia* crew decided to sail both ships to **Gibraltar**, at the tip of **Spain**. That was just enough men for one ship! Stretched to their limits, they barely made it, pulling into port on, of all days, Friday the 13th.

Hearings and investigations filled the next three months. No evidence of pirates, mutiny, or murder could be found. And no survivors ever showed up. Unable to decide anything else, the judge awarded the *Dei Gratia* crew a reward for bringing in the abandoned ship.

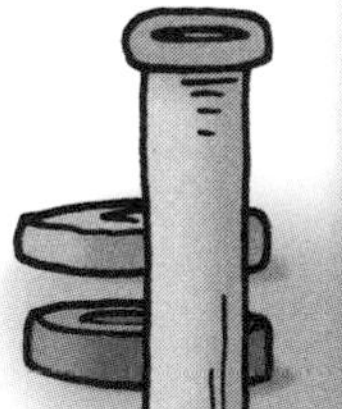

Sensational stories have been written for nearly a century and a half, but still, no one knows what happened to the 10 people aboard the *Mary Celeste*.

Mary Celeste means "heavenly Mary" and *Dei Gratia* means "grace of God."

iPuzzle

Sea-doku

 compass

 anchor

flag 

sailor's hat 

Draw in the missing pictures following the rules in the example.

All 4 pictures in each column

All 4 pictures in each row

All 4 pictures in each bold box

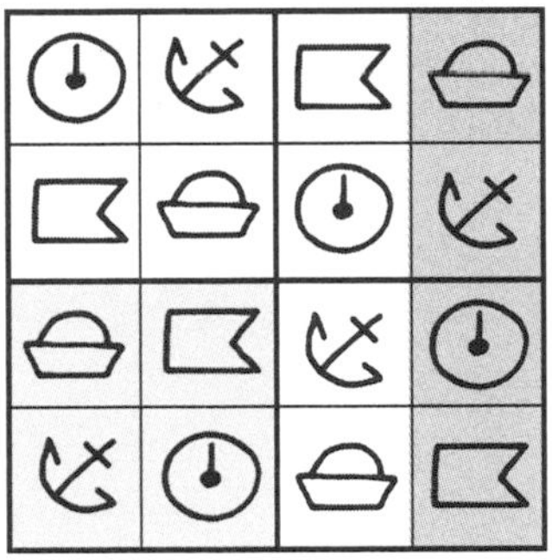

1.

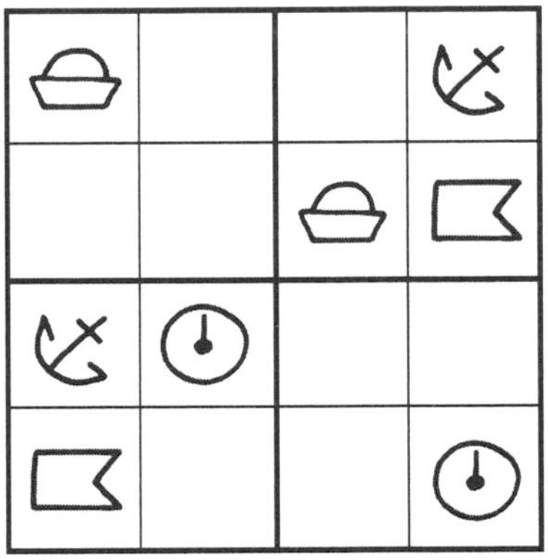

2.

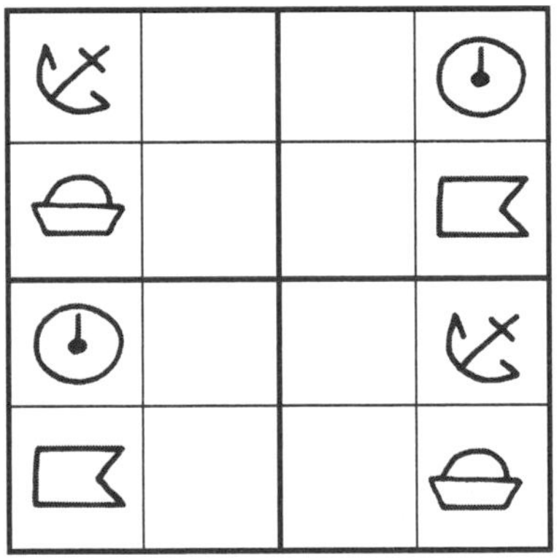

3.

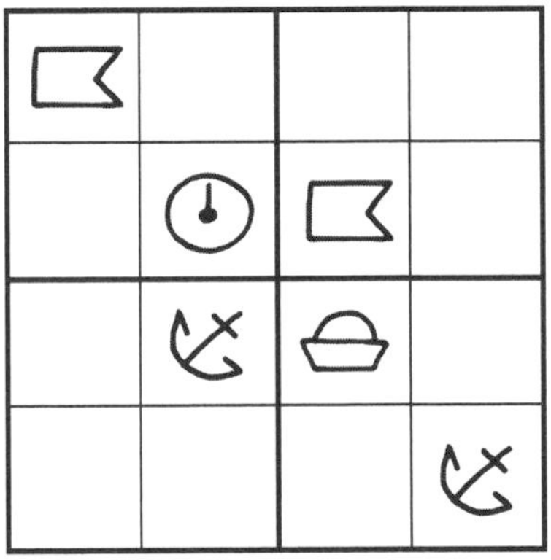

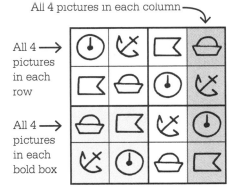

Jinxed: Bad luck continued for the *Mary Celeste* after its "haunted house" voyage. On a trip to Uruguay, its load of lumber tumbled overboard in a storm; and on the way to Mauritius (in the Indian Ocean), most of its cargo of horses died. Soon after, its captain died as well. The ship was sold several times, with each of its owners losing money.

Jump to this page **or** follow the pipes.

It's called J. Habakuk Jephson's Statement.

In 1884 Sir Arthur Conan Doyle, Sherlock Holmes's creator, wrote a story about the *Mary Celeste.*

1960 **Where:** The National Radio Astronomy Observatory in Green Bank, West Virginia

Out There

Are we alone in the universe? For centuries, people have reported seeing UFOs or meeting visitors from other planets. But aliens have yet to land in **Times Square** or at **Disneyland**, where there would be lots of witnesses and cameras. So the rest of us are left wondering.

Hoping to change that, an astronomer named **Frank Drake** started **Project Ozma**. From April to July in 1960, he aimed the **world's largest radio telescope** at two nearby stars, **Epsilon Eridani** and **Tau Ceti**. He then listened for any sign of intelligent life. And? Nothing. No radio or TV shows, not even an unexplainable string of beeps or bloops.

The next year, Drake shifted his focus—trying to figure out just how much intelligent life might be lurking out amongst the stars. He used a mathematical approach, which he called the **Drake Equation**.

Each step in the equation (see next page) narrows down the possibilities, until all that's left is the number of planets in our **galaxy** that might be able to communicate with us.

The problem is, it gets complicated figuring out what numbers to use. For example, how do you decide what kind of planet can support life (#3 in the puzzle)? People used to think life couldn't exist in a freezing cold, totally dark, or oxygenless environment. But that's all been proven wrong right here on Earth.

Still, in 1961 Drake and a small group of other curious scientists made a stab at coming up with an answer to the Drake Equation. Their result—there could be 5,000 civilizations out there, just waiting to talk to us!

Some doubters using the Drake Equation come up with an answer of zero.
Others end up with huge numbers.

For more about life that exists in extreme environments, see "Extremophiles" in *iFlush: Swimming in Science.* ...

... Epsilon Eridani and Tau Ceti are about 70 trillion miles (112 trillion km) from Earth.

iPuzzle

The Drake Equation

It's your turn to figure out how much life there might be in our galaxy. (We've included Frank Drake's 1961 numbers in blue.)

First, fill in your numbers.

1. How many stars do you think are created each year? (10) ______

2. What percentage of stars have planets orbiting them? (50%) ______%

3. How many planets (orbiting an average star) can support life? (1) ______

4. What percentage of life-supporting planets *do* develop life? (10%) ______%

5. What percentage of planets with life have intelligent life? (100%) ______%

6. What percentage of intelligent-life planets have communication technology we can detect? (100%) ______%

7. How many years can a planet with communication technology continue to have it? (10,000) ________

Next, get out a calculator and multiply all the numbers together:

______ × ______ × ______ × ______ × ______ × ______ × ________ = ________

Drake: 10 × 50% × 1 × 10% × 100% × 100% × 10,000 = 5,000

What songs are sung on Neptune.
Neptunes.

Looking for Life: It's not just scientist types who think life might exist elsewhere. The followers of some religions believe God could have created other intelligent beings. But should we seek them out? According to the physicist Stephen Hawking—no! He thinks it would likely end in disaster, with superior beings raiding our planet.

Year:
1968
Page:
10
Go
Return

Jump to this page **or** follow the pipes.

1888 **Where:** Georgia, Michigan, and Kentucky, to sample some tasty treats. But, shhh, don't tell anyone…

It's a Secret!

Many companies get very quiet when it comes to how their products are made. Here's a tight-lipped trio.

Coca-Cola: When **Asa Candler** bought Coca-Cola in 1888, about 10 other people knew how to make it. He took care of that by changing the recipe and telling only his partner. Then, to keep the ingredients secret from his workers, he removed the package labels and numbered them 1 through 9. Candler also handled the mail and bills himself so no one else would know what he was buying. Coke's secret formula is now locked in a vault in **Atlanta, Georgia**.

Kellogg's Corn Flakes: In 1894 the Kellogg brothers created flaked cereal as a **health food** at their vegetarian resort in **Michigan**. Competitors started copying them almost immediately, but it wasn't until 1986 that the company stopped giving tours at their factory. Why? Spies from rival companies kept getting in line, as many as 20 times each, to see how to make the stuff.

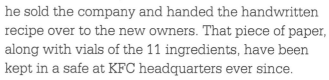

↓ Sanders's original restaurant, Sanders Cafe, with a 1980s KFC sign behind it; photo by Brent Moore

KFC: In 1940 **Colonel Harland Sanders** concocted a "secret blend of 11 herbs and spices" to coat his fried chicken. He shared it only with his wife until 1964 when he sold the company and handed the handwritten recipe over to the new owners. That piece of paper, along with vials of the 11 ingredients, have been kept in a safe at KFC headquarters ever since.

In a 1974 article for ***Esquire*** magazine, a panel of chefs tried to figure out what went into the mix, but couldn't agree. As for the employees at KFC's more than 18,000 restaurants, they have no idea what's in it, either. The powder is sent to them premixed.

Two of the most understood terms in the world: OK and Coca-Cola.

iPuzzle

Label Maker

Piece these labels back together. Write the letters in the squares, or draw in the pieces.

1. Use pieces A–E

Coca-Cola

Carbonated water, sucrose,

A

2. Use pieces F–N

Kellogg's Co

Ingredients: Mille

malt fla

salt. BH

freshne

Iron, vit

3. Use pieces O–X

Origi

Fresh c

Salt, so

monoso

with: W

and ant

A.

B. id,

C. sphoric ac
ffeine.

D. l color, pho
flavors, ca

E. caramel
natural

F. B6, vitami
A palmita
D, vitami

G. es
gar,

H. n B2, vita
te, folic ac
B12.

I. nin B1,
id,

J. ns 2% or l
o packagi
s and Min
acinamide

K. vitamin
vitamin
vitamin

L. ess of
g for
erals:
,

M. vor, contai
T added t
ss. **Vitami**
amin C, ni

N. **rn Flak**
d corn, su

O. **ipe® Ch**
rinated wit

P. **aded**
loride
lcium

Q. **nal Rec**
hicken ma

R. ate), nonfa
Colonel's
easoning.

S. dium phos
dium glut
heat flour,
i-caking a

T. **icken**
h:

U. phate and
amate. **Bre**
sodium c
gent (trica

V. t milk, eg
secret orig

W. phosph
whites,
recipe s

X. g
inal

Jump to this page **or** follow the pipes.

The labels in the puzzle copy how those products list their ingredients, while still keeping the important details secret.

1982 **Where:** Guam, an island in the Pacific Ocean, eight hours west of Hawaii by plane

Tweet Free

Julie Savidge, a graduate student in **biology**, has just touched down on this tropical paradise. She's come to try to solve a mystery—why **Guam**'s birds are disappearing.

In 1970 more than a dozen bird species, some found nowhere else, lived here. But by 1980 the island's southern forests had become birdless. And the forests to the north weren't far behind. It seemed the work of some evil spirit, making birds vanish as it moved slowly up the island. Poof! But Savidge knew it was something more real than that.

She ruled out bug-killing sprays, overhunting, wild cats and dogs, storms, habitat loss, and competition from non-native birds such as **drongos** and **francolins**. What was left? Disease, the experts concluded.

Savidge wasn't so sure. After talking with the locals, she suspected a slithering island intruder, the **brown tree snake**, might be to blame. "Preposterous!" the experts said. A **reptile** couldn't eat up an entire island of birds. It had never been seen. Anywhere. Ever.

Step by step, like a detective, Savidge went to work. Slowly, a picture emerged of an island writhing in ornery snakes—over a million of them! They'd come here accidentally in the '50s, aboard a vessel from another island, then gradually taken over.

Nothing could stop them. They slinked into underground nests and climbed to the highest tree branches, along power lines, and up cliff walls. They could even launch themselves through the air. Egad!

Unfortunately, by 1986, when Savidge finally convinced everyone that brown tree snakes were the culprits, it was far too late. The serpents had already wiped out nine native bird species.

Since the disappearance of Guam's birds, the spider population has increased 40 times over.

Brown tree snakes range in length from about two feet (.5 m) to nearly ten (3 m).

iPuzzle

Bird Watching

The names of nine birds that once lived on Guam have been anagrammed (the letters rearranged) to spell nonsense phrases. Can you match them up?

1. ___ FOUL NUT SAFARI

2. ___ BAD GORILLA BUM

3. ___ WIRY-HIDED BEETLE

4. ___ INCREASING HEROISM FINK

5. ___ A GLUM AIR

6. ___ AROUND TRIVIA FAME

7. ___ NATIONAL CHEERER DAY

8. ___ THROWING REDHEAD OUTVOTED

9. ___ LIGHTER BAGEL DINNERWARE

A. MARIANA FRUIT-DOVE
B. GUAM RAIL
C. RUFOUS FANTAIL
D. MICRONESIAN KINGFISHER
E. NIGHTINGALE REED-WARBLER
F. CARDINAL HONEYEATER
G. WHITE-THROATED GROUND-DOVE
H. BRIDLED WHITE-EYE
I. GUAM BROADBILL

Raining Mice: Four times in 2013, the U.S. Dept. of Agriculture parachuted 2,000 dead mice onto Guam. Hidden inside each of the critters was an acetaminophen tablet (that's like Tylenol), which is deadly to brown tree snakes. More mice drops will follow if the pill-filled snacks prove effective in reducing the island's snake population.

Jump to this page **or** follow the pipes.

Brown tree snakes on Guam also eat tons of lizards, cats, rodents, chickens, and eggs.

2014 **Where:** The White House, in Washington, D.C.

Do Not Enter!

I'm outside the **White House** fence. But that's as far as I'm going—I don't want to get nuked! Sure, a few people have made it onto the grounds in the past, but who knows what's been installed since then.

Some of the White House defenses are obvious, like this superstrong iron fence. Also, I can see officers standing at the gates, agents roaming the grounds, and snipers on the White House roof. But the **Secret Service**, the agency that protects the president, has one answer when asked about other security measures they use: No comment.

Are there **missile launchers** on top of the White House? Some people think so, to shoot down enemy planes. But would the Secret Service really want a plane crashing in the middle of Washington, D.C.? And what if the missiles accidentally hit a building instead?

To avoid that possibility, **air traffic controllers** now track every plane in the U.S. Any intruder entering the **restricted air space** around the White House ⟶ gets a warning of brightly flashing red and green laser beams, before being escorted away by **F-16 fighter jets**.

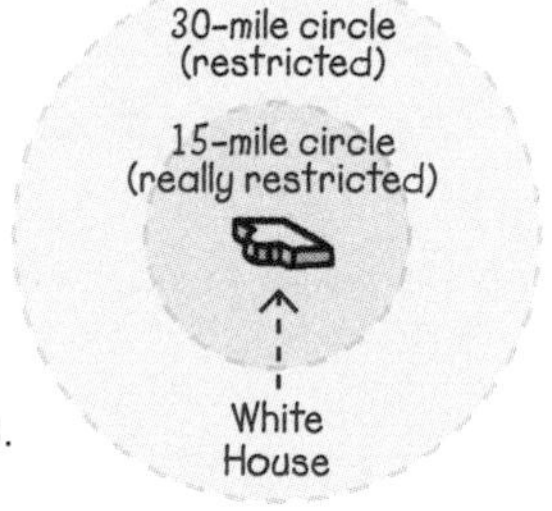

What's under the White House? During **World War II**, a bomb shelter was built six stories below the **East Wing**. It was later outfitted with communication equipment so it could serve as an emergency command center. In 2010 workers dug a huge hole next to the **West Wing** (where the president works). Officially, it was to replace utility systems, but some suspect it was part of a project to enlarge the underground command center.

Do tunnels and underground trains exist to evacuate the president during an emergency? That'd be really cool if it were true, but that one's still a big question mark.

In 1943 FDR flew to Casablanca, the first time a U.S. president traveled by airplane while in office. ...

Casablanca means "white house" in Spanish.

iPuzzle

The Prez

The Secret Service uses code names for the presidents. First, guess whose code name is whose, then follow the lines to see if you're right.

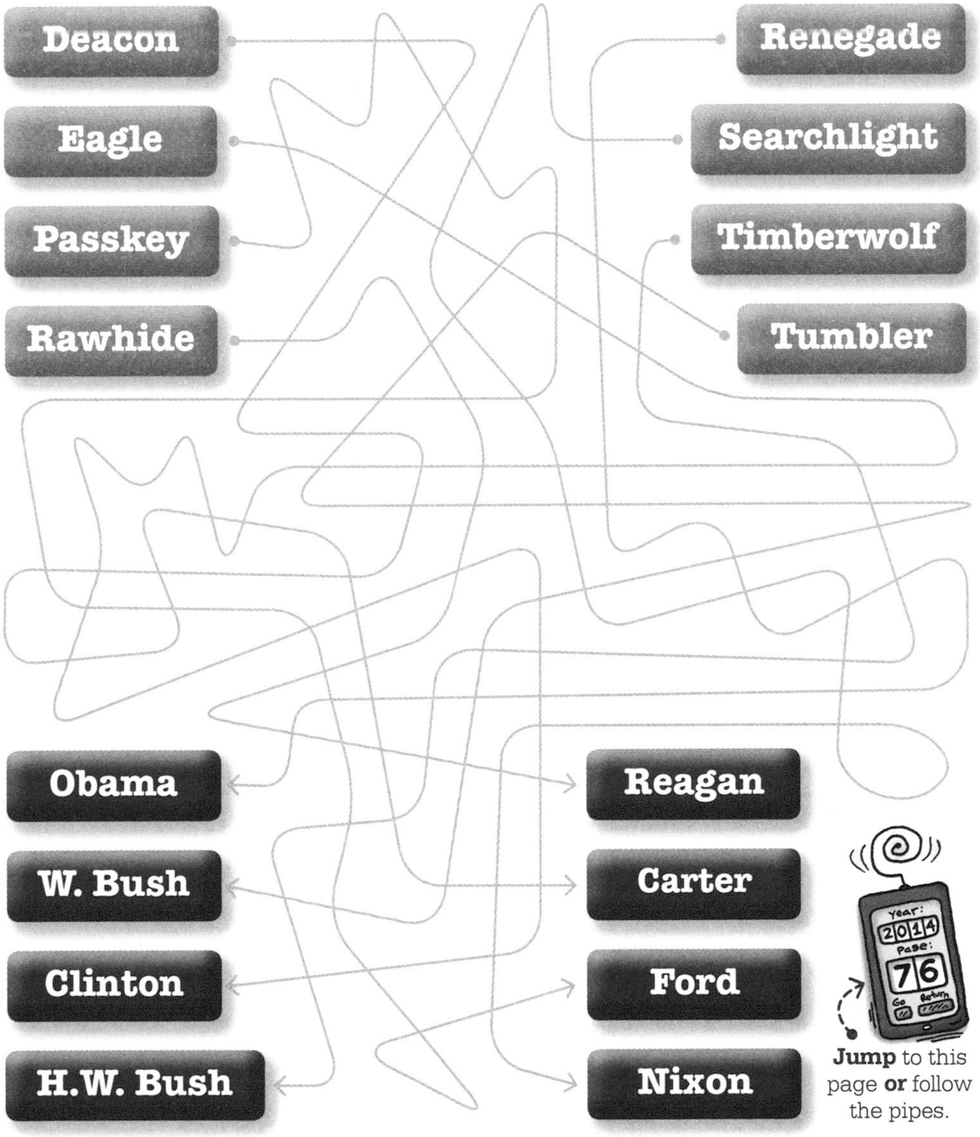

Jump to this page **or** follow the pipes.

Smurfette was the code name given to Karenna Gore, one of Vice President Al Gore's daughters.

Abraham Lincoln created the Secret Service only a few hours before he was assassinated.

1795 **Where:** Mahone Bay, a small town on a bay of the same name in southern Nova Scotia, Canada

The Money Pit

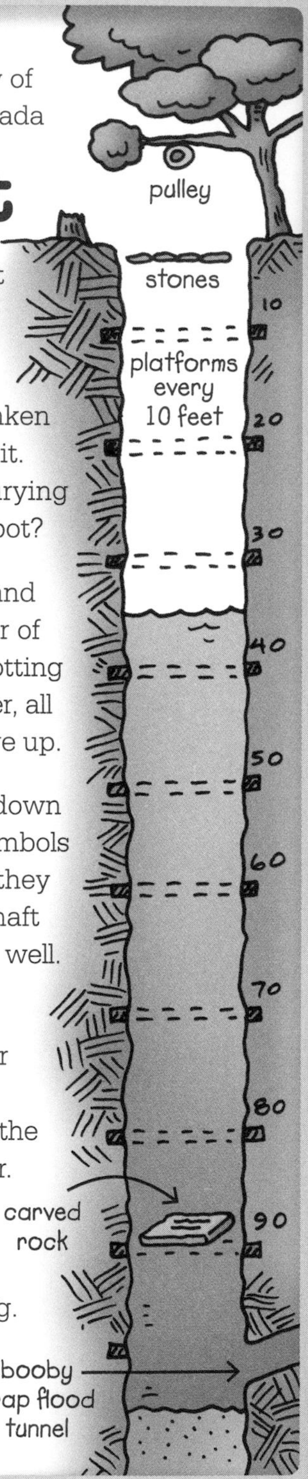

It's nighttime, and a teenager named **Daniel McGinnis** sat peering out a window in his house. What's he looking at? A strange light coming from **Oak Island** across the bay.

The next day, Daniel rowed to the island and noticed a sunken area in the ground. A pulley hung from a tree branch above it. Tales had been told of **Captain Kidd**, the famous pirate, burying his treasure on the **Nova Scotia** coast. Could this be the spot?

Daniel returned with two friends and an armload of picks and shovels. After digging down two feet (.6 m), they hit a layer of **flagstones**. At 10 feet (3 m), they uncovered a platform of rotting logs. Surely, something lurked below. But as they dug deeper, all they found was dirt and more log platforms. They finally gave up.

In 1803 the **Oslow Company** resumed the dig. At 90 feet down (27 m), they discovered a rectangular rock with strange symbols carved into it (see puzzle). Although they couldn't read it, they excitedly dug on. Eight feet later, a **booby trap** filled the shaft with water. Their spirits dampened, that group soon quit as well.

Over the years, more treasure hunters took on the "Money Pit," as it came to be known. They tried pumping the water out, drilling, and digging parallel shafts. Nothing worked. When one group discovered a tunnel feeding seawater into the pit, they attempted to plug it up. But that didn't work, either.

Six men lost their lives digging on Oak Island. The most disastrous day came in 1965, when four men died from inhaling poisonous gas leaking out of a new shaft they'd dug.

So, what's in the pit? Nobody knows...but only because someone went to a lot of trouble to keep it that way.

Remove AH and BA from MAHONE BAY and you're left with... MONEY.

Coconut fibers have been found in the Money Pit, nowhere near where coconut trees grow.

iPuzzle

The Rock

A rock with symbols on it was dug up on Oak Island in 1803. The one below is supposedly it, decoded by Professor James Leitchi in the 1860s. Use the key to discover its secret message.

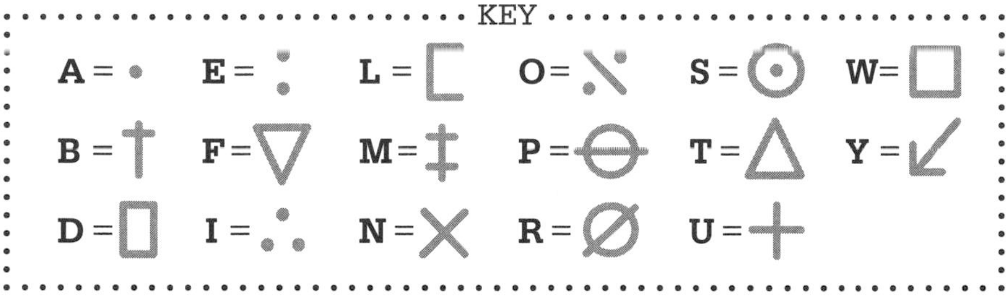

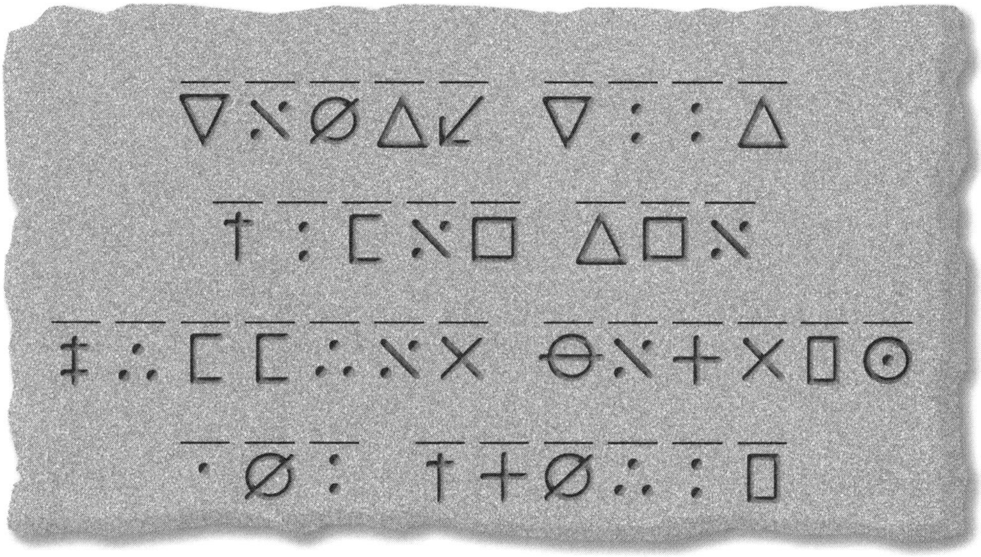

FDR: In the summer of 1910, 24 years before he became a U.S. president, Franklin Roosevelt came to Oak Island to dig for treasure. He was an investor in the Old Gold Salvage and Wrecking Company.

Jump to this page **or** follow the pipes.

The phrase *money pit* has come to mean any project that costs more and more money.

As much as $10 million has been spent trying to find treasure in Oak Island's Money Pit.

1999 **Where:** iFlush Labs, on the day that Plumb Bob first set eyes on the iSwirl

Don't Look at this Page

Oops, too late! Okay, just skip this part. Crikey, too late for that, too!

Both of those impossible-to-obey instructions are examples of **paradoxes**. They involve opposite ideas that make your brain go in circles. To illustrate another paradox, I've traveled back in time, taking the original **iSwirl** time-travel device with me. When **Plumb Bob** first saw it in 1999, he had no idea what it was. Several years later, the **Four P's** discovered what it could do…and then let me use it.

So where did the iSwirl come from? Ha! Paradox!

Don't worry, I'm only going to include five more paradox examples. Which of these ten should I use? Ha! Paradox!

1. Everything I say is false.

2. This box is intentionally blank.

3. You'll receive a pop quiz tomorrow, but only if you're not expecting it.

4. A law student agrees to pay her teacher, but only if she wins her first case. The teacher then sues her for payment, creating her first case.

5. I'll join your club but only if you don't accept me as a member.

6. How to stay cool:
a. Don't move.
b. Fan yourself.

7. "Follow no rules" is the only rule I follow.

8. If we never talk again, please let me know.

9. Today is opposite day. Do everything the opposite of how it should be done.

10. Nobody goes to that restaurant because it's always too crowded.

Paradox means "contrary to expectation" in Latin.

iPuzzle

Paradox

My brain is worn out. I hope this all ends sooner than it does!

Below are explanations for the 10 paradoxes on the previous page. Can you match them up?

A. ____ If you fan yourself, you'll move.

B. ____ But once you tell me, we will have talked again.

C. ____ If doing things the opposite way is how things should be done today, should I do things normally, the opposite of how things should be done?

D. ____ If nobody goes, how can it still be crowded?

E. ____ So that statement is false, which means everything I say is true?

F. ____ Since I'm now expecting it, there won't be a quiz. But now that I know there won't be a quiz, it would come as a surprise if one were given.

G. ____ But "Follow no rules" is a rule, and you don't follow rules.

H. ____ By adding the note, the box is no longer blank.

I. ____ If the student loses, that means she has to pay… but she can't, because she just lost her first case. If she wins, she's proven she doesn't have to pay… but she does, because she just won her first case.

J. ____ If you're allowed to join the club, you can't join.

The red button is blue.

Okay, so which button is red and which is blue?

The blue button is red.

Jump to this page **or** follow the pipes.

1518

Where: The city of Strasbourg in the Alsace region (later part of France)

Crazy Legs

It's a hot July day, and a peasant woman named **Frau Troffea** is dancing wildly in the street. Why? She's the city's first **dancing plague** victim.

At first, people didn't know what to make of Frau Troffea's trancelike jig. But when she continued almost nonstop for six days, they became scared. Was it the curse of a witch? Or the devil? Or God! They carted her off to the shrine of **St. Vitus** in nearby **Saverne**, hoping the priests there could cure her. But the foot-stomping sickness had spread, and 30 others now waltzed uncontrollably in Strasbourg's streets.

The town leaders called an emergency meeting and concluded that "overheated blood" was to blame. The cure? More dancing, to burn off the bad blood! The zombie-like dancers were herded into four public spaces where hired musicians and donated food would help keep them going.

How'd that work out? It didn't. The number of dancers soon grew to 100, then 400. Even worse, some of them began collapsing to the floor...dead.

The dance floors were quickly shut down. On top of that, the city passed a law making it illegal to dance in public, to avoid spreading the plague.

Still, the dancing plague continued to claim victims behind closed doors. A few weeks later, the town leaders ordered all the dancers taken to Saverne. Time and the caring attention of the priests seemed to do the trick. By the end of August, there were no new cases, and the last of the survivors had snapped out of it.

So what caused the dancing plague of 1518? Some have suggested it was stress from years of extreme poverty and famine. Others pointed to spiritual forces or even poisoning from rye mold. But, to this day, nobody's quite sure.

Men, women, and children alike fell victim to the dancing plague of 1518.

Choreomania is the formal term for uncontrollable dancing.

iPuzzle

May I Cut In?

Which two pieces *don't* exactly match squares in this "dancing plague" engraving by Henrik Hondius, from a drawing by Pieter Bruegel the Elder?

1.

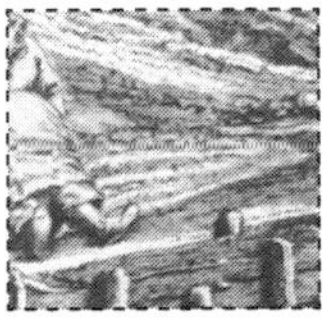

2.

3.

4.

5.

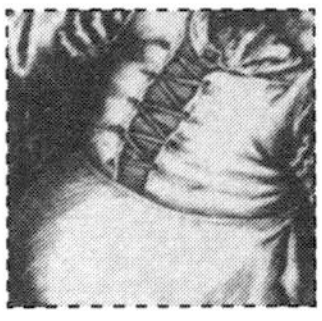

6.

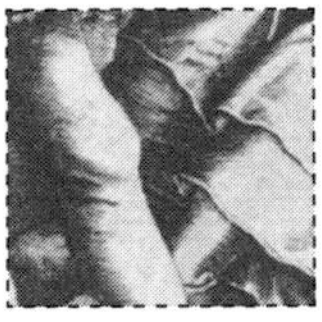

7.

8.

Jump to this page **or** follow the pipes.

In 1962 a laughing plague hit several villages in Tanzania, Africa, lasting more than two years.

1672

Where: In Europe to visit Ireland and France, then off to India and back to North Africa

Wild Child

Many tales have been told of children raised by wild animals. Are they true? Some people claim these five are.

Sheep Boy: In 1672 hunters in **Ireland** netted a boy thought to have been raised by sheep. They said he looked about 16 and acted more like a wild beast than a human. He preferred eating grass and hay and could only make sheep sounds. *Baa!*

Savage Girl: In 1731 the villagers of **Songi, France**, spotted a dark-skinned girl in the woods who looked about 10 years old. She ran in galloping strides, carried a wooden club, and dug for roots in the ground. After luring her in, the villagers were amazed to discover her skin was pale white, covered in dirt and paint. They named her Memmie le Blanc (White Memmie).

Leopard Boy: In 1912 in **Assam, India**, a small boy was stolen from his parents by a female leopard. By the time he was found, three years later, his knees, feet, and palms had become callused from running on all fours. He'd also become a dangerous hunter. If allowed to get close enough to a chicken, he'd grab the unsuspecting bird and eat it raw.

Wolf Girls: In 1920 two young girls were pulled from a wolf den in **Godamuri, India**. Given the names **Amala** and **Kamala**, they slept during the day as wolves do and became active at night, sometimes howling. They had also developed especially sharp senses of hearing and smell.

Ostrich Boy: In 1945, at age five, **Sidi Mohamed** says he wandered off from his family in **North Africa** and befriended an ostrich family. For the next 10 years he lived with them, running, eating grass, and sleeping under their wings at night.

A few other animals credited with raising human children: bears, goats, monkeys, dogs, and pigs.

Children raised in the wild, with no human contact, are called *feral children*.

iPuzzle

Tarzan of the Apes

Tarzan, an English boy raised by apes, first appeared in a 1912 story. He inspired another famous hero, first seen in 1933 and also raised by unusual creatures. To find out who it is, follow the step-by-step directions.

1. Start with TARZAN... TARZAN

2. Write the letters in reverse order... ____________

3. Remove AT... ____________

4. Add ES to the end... ____________

5. Change the Z to an M... ____________

6. Reverse the letter order again... ____________

7. Insert UP after the S... ____________

The "unusual creatures" are identified in the answer section.

Now follow the directions to discover the name of Tarzan's ape mother:

1. Again, start with TARZAN... TARZAN

2. Change RZ to L... ____________

3. Remove the T... ____________

4. Reverse the letter order... ____________

5. Change the N to K... ____________

Mythical Wolf Boys: According to Roman mythology, the twin brothers Romulus and Remus were abandoned at birth. A she-wolf then nursed them and a woodpecker fed them. The twins later went on to create the city of Rome.

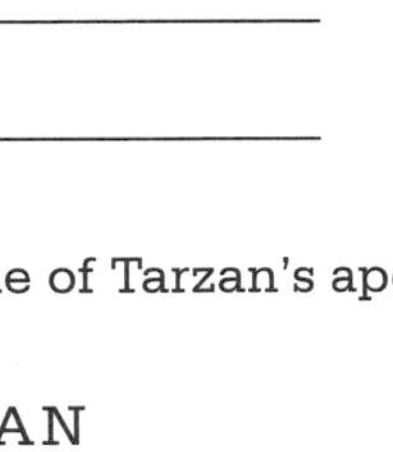

Jump to this page **or** follow the pipes.

In Rudyard Kipling's *The Jungle Book*, the main character, Mowgli, is raised by wolves.

1958

Where: Aboard a B-47 bomber on a practice combat mission over Tybee Island near Savannah, Georgia

Bombs Away

KA-BLAAASH! Yikes, we hit something. Out the window I can see an **F-86** fighter jet going down and its pilot ejecting. We're not in much better shape, so the crew has gotten permission to shove a **hydrogen bomb** out the door to lighten our load. You read that right! The bomb, equal to two million tons of TNT, will splash unexploded into **Wassaw Sound**, never to be seen again.

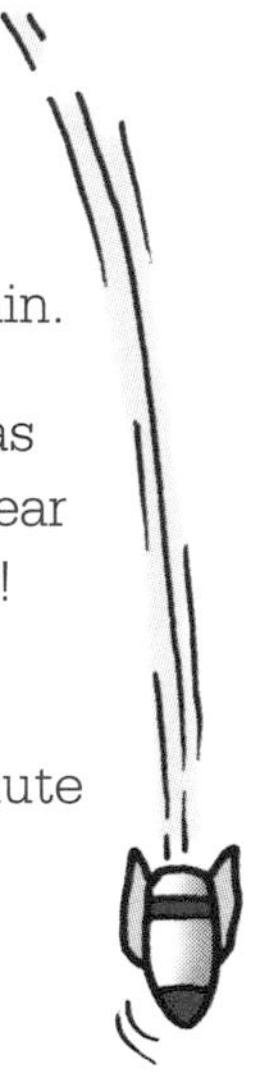

Amazingly, today isn't the only time something like this has happened. Over the years, the U.S. has officially lost 11 nuclear bombs in accidents, but the unofficial guess is closer to 50!

In 1961, near **Goldsboro, North Carolina**, a faulty fuel line exploded on a **B-52 bomber**. The crew managed to parachute one of the aircraft's two hydrogen bombs safely into a tree. But the other plunged at full speed into a swamp, where it remains buried half a football field down in the muck.

In 1965, not far from **Japan**, an **A-4 Skyhawk** aircraft rolled off the side of the aircraft carrier **USS** ***Ticonderoga***. It sank to the ocean bottom, too far down to retrieve its one-ton nuclear weapon.

In 1966, along the southeast coast of **Spain**, a B-52 bomber crashed into a **tanker aircraft** while attempting to refuel in midair. Both planes exploded, causing two of the B-52's four hydrogen bombs to partially detonate. Bomb fragments and radioactive dust rained down on the coastal city of **Palomares**. The third bomb landed safely in a tomato field, and the last disappeared in the **Mediterranean Sea**.

In 1968, in the middle of the **Atlantic Ocean**, the nuclear sub **USS** ***Scorpion*** sank in a still-unexplained accident. The crew, a nuclear reactor, and two nuclear-warhead torpedoes were lost, coming to rest 10,800 feet (3,300 m) below the surface.

Hydrogen bomb is sometimes shortened to H-bomb.

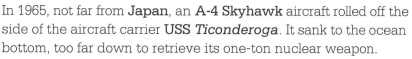

In 1952 the first hydrogen-bomb test totally eliminated Elugelab, an island in the Pacific.

iPuzzle

Missing Bomb

Each answer below is missing the letters B-O-M-B, *in any order*. Use the clues to help you figure out the words and phrases.

Soft squishy ball material	**1.**	F ___ A ___ RU ___ ___ ER
One who lets secrets slip	**2.**	___ LAB ___ ER ___ ___ UTH
One of the Four P's	**3.**	PLU ___ ___ ___ ___ B
Plant eaten by pandas	**4.**	___ A ___ ___ ___ O
Library on wheels	**5.**	___ O ___ K ___ O ___ ILE
Pants with flared legs	**6.**	___ ELL- ___ ___ TTO ___ S
Jam-packed with people	**7.**	___ ___ ___ ___ ED
Nonsense	**8.**	___ UM ___ O JUM ___ ___
Very unlikely	**9.**	I ___ PR ___ ___ A ___ LE
Old nursery-rhyme woman whose cupboard was bare	**10.**	___ ___ THER HU ___ ___ ARD

Look at page 6 if you forget their names.

EXTRA CREDIT

Member of the generation born in the late '40s–early '60s	**11.**	___ A ___ Y BO ___ ___ ER

Bomb Code: In the early '70s, secret codes were required to launch nuclear-warhead missiles at the Strategic Air Command in Omaha, Nebraska. But according to one officer who worked there, Bruce G. Blair, the unlock codes were all set to 00000000. The reason—the workers didn't want any complications if a launch order came through. That was finally changed in 1977.

Jump to this page **or** follow the pipes.

The Davy Crockett, one of the smallest nuclear weapons, could be launched from a rifle on a tripod.

1828 **Where:** Nan Madol, a tight cluster of 90 or so islets off the coast of Pohnpei, a Pacific island

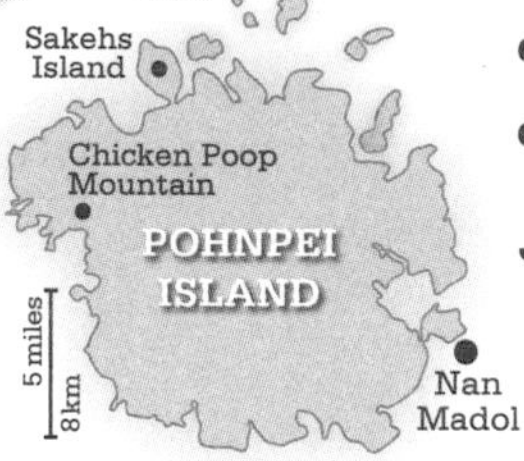

Lava Land

Basalt is a rock formed by the rapid cooling of lava.

James O'Connell, a shipwrecked Irish sailor, has just discovered this strange city of tiny islands. How strange? It's man-made.

Local islanders who have befriended O'Connell are trying to stop him from going in. "*Acoa ban midjila!*" they howl, "You will die!" They believe evil spirits live in **Nan Madol**. But O'Connell ignores their warnings and paddles his canoe through its **canals**. The humongous stone buildings on the islets, all abandoned, are unlike anything he's ever seen!

The construction method is similar to how **log cabins** are made. Workers stacked a frame of **basalt** "logs" on top of the **coral reef** that surrounds Pohnpei. Then they filled in the frame with coral rubble to make an islet. Many more logs were stacked atop the islets to make the buildings.

Who created Nan Madol? Legend has it that twin brothers, **Olisihpa** and **Olosohpa**, came to **Pohnpei** hundreds of years ago. They built the city in one day, using a **dragon** to cut through the coral and magic to lift the logs.

Looking at these buildings, made of stone logs and boulders weighing up to *50 tons each*, that legend begins to sound a little less crazy. The nearest known basalt sources are on **Sakehs Island** or at **Pwisehn Malek** (translation: Chicken Poop Mountain). Dragging the stone logs through the thick jungle or transporting them on rafts seems equally impossible. And how did the workers raise them up to make 30-foot-high walls (10 meters)? You got me!

In 1833 O'Connell was rescued by the U.S. ship ***Spy of Salem***. He soon shared his story with the world, the first written account of Nan Madol. But who built this city, as well as when and how, still remains a secret.

. . Because of its canals, Nan Madol has been called the "Venice of the Pacific." . . .

Nan Madol required 250 million tons of stone, about 40 times as much as the Great Pyramid of Giza.

iPuzzle

Canoe Find It?

Follow the directions to find your way to Nan Dowas islet, home to Nan Madol's largest building.

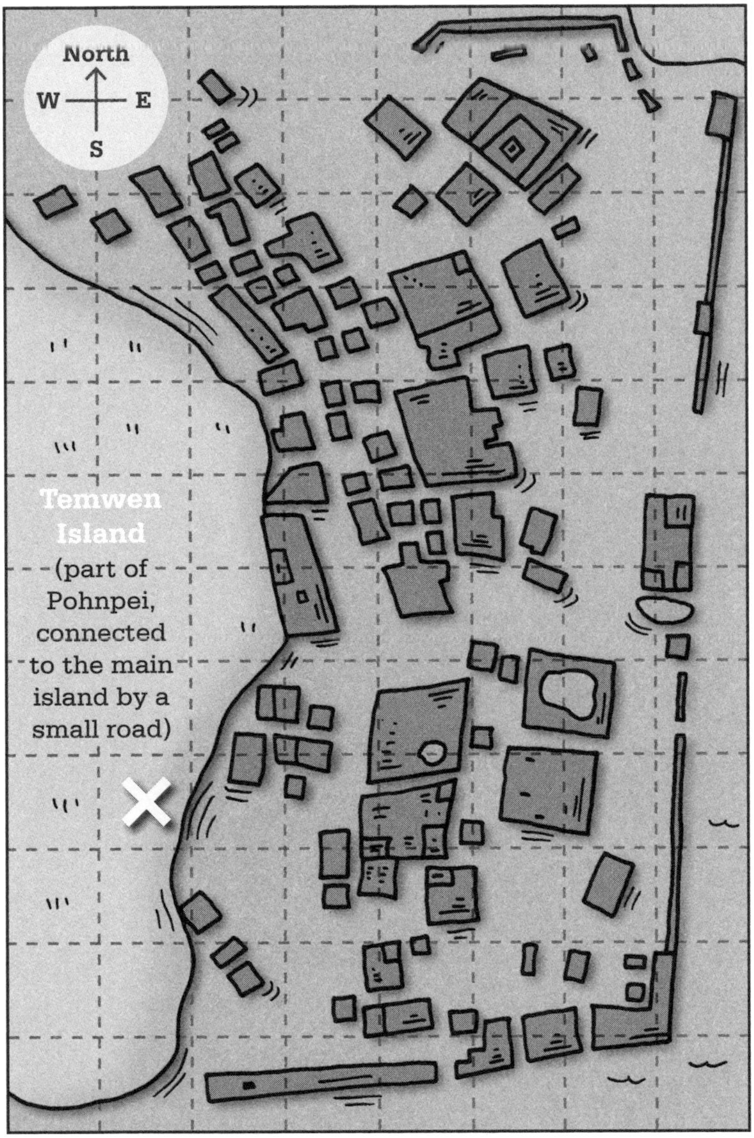

Start at ✕ on Temwen Island

1. Paddle EAST 2 squares
2. Go NORTH 2 squares
3. Go EAST 3 squares
4. Go NORTH 6 squares
5. Go WEST 3 squares
6. Go SOUTH 2 squares
7. Go EAST 2 squares
8. Go NORTH 1 square

Welcome to Nan Dowas!

Jump to this page **or** follow the pipes.

Strangers known as Sandeleurs ruled Nan Madol for about 400 years, driven out by islanders perhaps in the 1400's.

Some of Nan Madol's buildings were used for sacrificing turtles or for housing sacred eels.

1997 **Where:** The Pacific Marine Environmental Laboratory in Newport, Oregon

The Bloop

The scientists at this lab spend a lot of time listening to the ocean. They don't put a seashell to their ears the way I would. They use hydrophones, underwater microphones that sit on the bottom of oceans around the world.

Today, they heard a really weird sound in the **South Pacific**, something they couldn't identify. It was long and slow and loud, an eerie noise that resembled...well, a huge bloop. So that's what they named it—**the Bloop**.

Some people think the Bloop sounds like a noise an animal would make. But here's the thing—if it was, the animal would have to be ENORMOUS because the sound was picked up by hydrophones placed 3,000 miles (5,000 km) apart! A giant squid or the largest whale couldn't come anywhere close to making a bellow that big.

Adding to the intrigue, science-fiction fans pointed out that the Bloop came from a location near the mythical sunken city of **R'yleh**, a 1928 creation of **H.P. Lovecraft**. According to his story, the **Cthulhu**, an octopus-headed monster as tall as the **Empire State Building**, was imprisoned there.

The Bloop wasn't the only strange sound scientists heard in 1997. Hydrophones picked up three more unidentifiable sounds they nicknamed **Train**, **Slow Down**, and **Whistle**.

In 2013 the **National Oceanic and Atmospheric Administration** (NOAA) finally announced an explanation for the mysterious blurbles below. Studying undersea ice off **Antarctica**, they concluded that the Bloop matched the sound of an **icequake**, the cracking of an ice shelf as it sent another iceberg out into the world.

The array of hydrophones in the world's oceans is known as SOSUS, short for Sound Surveillance System.

The U.S. Navy installed the hydrophones in the '60s for listening to Soviet subs.

iPuzzle

Oops!

Like BLOOP, each answer below contains O-O-P (sometimes with other letters in between). To solve, read a clue in the left column. Then see if you can complete a word in the right column that matches it.

1. _G_ Sagging	A. ___ ___ O O P ___
2. ___ Red-headed bird	B. ___ O ___ ___ ___ ___ O P
3. ___ Without interruption	C. ___ O O ___ ___ P ___ ___ ___
4. ___ Charlie Brown's dog	D. ___ ___ ___ ___ - ___ O O P
5. ___ Dog do picker-upper	E. ___ ___ ___ ___ O ___ ___ O P ___
6. ___ Scientist's enlarger	F. ___ O ___ O P ___ ___ ___
7. ___ Swiveling hips toy	G. _D_ _R_ O O P _I_ _N_ _G_
8. ___ Board game with a GO space	H. ___ O O ___ P ___ ___ ___ ___ ___
	I. ___ O ___ ___ ___ O P
9. ___ Sucker you lick	J. ___ O O P ___ ___ / ___ ___ O O P ___ ___ (Two-word phrase)
10. ___ Restaurant freebie resembling a splinter	

EXTRA-EXTRA CREDIT

11. Way of thinking about life: ___ ___ ___ ___ O ___ O P ___ ___

Hummmm: Two out of every 100 people who live in Taos, New Mexico, can hear a faint but constant hum. They describe it as sounding like an engine idling far, far away. Earplugs do no good, and some say it's louder indoors than out. Scientists have yet to find the source of the sound.

Jump to this page **or** follow the pipes.

The source of a sound recorded by the NOAA in 1991, named Upsweep, is still uncertain.

1916 **Where:** Albany, New York, down to North Carolina, across the pond to Ireland, then back to Florida

Sixth Sense

Can people predict the future, read thoughts, or move objects with their minds? So far, no scientific tests have been able to prove any of these **paranormal abilities**, but that hasn't stopped people from wondering.

Paratrivia: In 1916 **Charles Fort** inherited enough money from his uncle to quit working. He then spent most of his time collecting real-life examples of paranormal events and compiling them in books. At one point, he had notes on 40,000 unexplained experiences, including teleportation, alien sightings, moving objects mentally, defying gravity, and humans who could transform into animals, such as wolves and gorillas.

Zener cards used in Rhine's tests

ESP: In 1931 **J. B. Rhine** conducted a series of tests at **Duke University** trying to identify people with **extrasensory perception** (ESP). One student, **Adam Linzmayer**, did well in a card-guessing test—scoring 40 percent correct, twice as well as chance. However, after Rhine added precautions to eliminate trickery, Linzmayer's results leveled out to just average.

OOBE: In 1943 **George N. M. Tyrrell** wrote a book called ***Apparitions***. Among other things, it explored **out-of-body experiences** (OOBEs), the sensation of floating outside your own body. It's estimated that one in 10 people will have at least one OOBE in their lifetime, but little is still known about it.

The Amazing Randi: James Randi has made a career out of poking holes in paranormal claims. In 1964 he offered a prize of $1,000 to anyone whose paranormal abilities could stand up to testing. He later upped it to $1 million. No one has collected.

Someone who uses scientific methods to analyze unusual events is called an *anomalist*.

Clairgustance is the ability to taste something new without putting it in your mouth.

iPuzzle

Mind Reader

Prove you can see into the future with this magic trick.

First, make a few preparations in secret:

1. Write the number 3 on a piece of paper and fold it over twice.

2. Remove all four 3's from a deck of cards and put them on top of the deck, facedown.

Now perform the trick for your audience:

3. Place the folded paper in sight for all to see, telling them you've written a prediction on it.

4. Deal the top FOUR cards (the 3's) into a pile, facedown.

5. Deal off the next THREE cards, making a second pile.

6. Deal off FIVE more cards into a third pile.

7. Now have an audience member point to one of the piles.

8. a. If the first pile is picked, turn over the four 3's and say, "Just as I predicted. I have written down the number three."

b. If the second pile is picked, point out that there are three cards and say, "Just as I predicted. I have written down the number three."

c. If the third pile is picked, say, "Pile number three. Just as I predicted. I have written down the number three."

9. Then unfold the paper and show them the number.

Jump to this page **or** follow the pipes.

A *poltergeist* ("noisy ghost" in German) is a ghost that can move things, often making loud noises.

1225 B.C. **Where:** The library of the Egyptian scribe (writer) Kenhirkhopeshef in the Valley of the Kings, Egypt

Dream On

I'm looking for one item in particular and…yes, here it is—a scroll known as the **Ramesside Dream Book**. It was written before Kenhirkhopeshef's time, but it's still being used by Egyptian bigwigs to interpret their dreams.

Dreams fascinated the **ancient Egyptians**. They saw them as predictions sent from the gods. This book lists over 200 dream images, rating each as being either a good or a bad sign. For example, plunging into a river is seen as good because it means one's evils will be washed away (see more examples in the puzzle on the next page).

The Egyptians weren't the only ones to write about dreams. All through history, people have been wondering what these "mind movies" are all about. They've come up with a lot of different explanations, such as…dreams are:

- journeys taken by one's soul
- a method for revealing illnesses in the body
- meaningless fantasies created by our brains
- a way to contact the dead

In the twentieth century, the psychiatrist **Sigmund Freud** chimed in, stating that dreams reflect our deepest desires, even those from childhood. A student of Freud's, **Carl Jung**, tweaked that to view dreams as messages from our inner selves, reminding us of what we want.

Scientific research in the twenty-first century suggests that dreams are the brain's way of sorting out all the information that flows into it. Important memories are stored, events are rerun, comparisons and connections are made, and new strategies might even be tried out.

What do I think? I think I need to sleep on it.

A newborn human baby dreams more than twice as much as an adult.

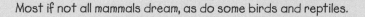

iPuzzle

Good or Bad?

Below are 11 images listed in the Ramesside Dream Book. To find out which are considered good signs and which are bad, do the math.

If the total is above 10, circle **GOOD**; below 10, circle **BAD**.

In a dream, if you...			above 10	below 10
...have dirt in your mouth	**1.**	7 + 13 - 9 = ____	GOOD	**BAD**
...are writing on paper	**2.**	6 + 9 ÷ 3 = ____	GOOD	**BAD**
...rub fat on yourself	**3.**	3 × 3 - 2 = ____	GOOD	**BAD**
...eat crocodile meat	**4.**	18 ÷ 3 + 5 = ____	GOOD	**BAD**
...put a bench in a boat	**5.**	2 × 7 - 6 = ____	GOOD	**BAD**
...have a bare butt	**6.**	2 + 4 + 3 = ____	GOOD	**BAD**
...see a snake	**7.**	8 × 3 ÷ 2 = ____	GOOD	**BAD**
...sit on top of a palm tree	**8.**	2 × 3 × 2 = ____	GOOD	**BAD**
...munch on lotus leaves	**9.**	12 - 9 × 4 = ____	GOOD	**BAD**
...have a leopard head	**10.**	10 × 2 - 7 = ____	GOOD	**BAD**
...see monkeys	**11.**	4 × 4 ÷ 2 = ____	GOOD	**BAD**

Cure: The Ramesside Dream Book provided a spell that could prevent bad dreams from coming true. First, rub a piece of bread scented with fresh herbs, beer, and thorn-tree oil on your face. Then call to the goddess Isis, starting with: "Come to me, come to me, O my mother Isis! Behold, I am seeing things which are far from my dwelling place!"

Jump to this page **or** follow the pipes.

Armadillos in captivity sleep 17 hours a day and spend up to 20 percent of that time dreaming.

1990

Where: The Isabella Stewart Gardner Museum in Boston, Massachusetts

Clipped Art

FBI sketch of the "cops"

It's dark, 2:45 in the morning, and I can just make out two **policemen** as they hustle out the side door of the **museum**. They throw armloads of stuff in the back of an unmarked vehicle, hop in, and take off.

What's going on? Those weren't cops—they were thieves in disguise! Back inside the museum, two **security guards** sit handcuffed in the basement with duct tape over their eyes and mouths. The two crooks have just made off with 13 pieces of art worth half a *billion* dollars!

Over the next few weeks, real policemen, museum officials, close to 30 **FBI** agents, and **Harold Smith**, a world-famous art detective with a black eyepatch and a rubber nose (due to cancer), swarmed in. A TV episode of ***America's Most Wanted*** showcased the robbery. The museum put up a $5 million reward. The result—zip. No arrests. No recovered art.

FBI reward poster

SEEKING INFORMATION
BY THE FBI
The Storm on the Sea of Galilee
REMBRANDT, 1633
$5 Million Reward

As the years passed, many tips came in, but they led nowhere. A few local thieves claimed to know where the art was, but they were lying, hoping to snag some of the reward. In desperation, the FBI hired **psychics**. Their visions of seeing the art hidden behind a brick wall in the museum or in a South American Indian village didn't pan out.

Finally, in 2013, the FBI announced it had identified the crooks. But since the time limit for charging anyone had run out, no arrests were made. The suspects' names remain a secret as agents continue to search for the art.

In the meantime, frames that once held the stolen art hang empty on the museum walls. Why? The museum's founder stated in her will that only her original collection of art could be displayed there.

The Gardner Museum robbery ranks as the biggest art theft ever.

iPuzzle

Concert-tration

Below is Vermeer's *The Concert*. Valued at $200 million, it was the biggest loss in the Gardner Museum theft. Study it closely for one minute, then see if you can answer eight questions about it on the next page.

The woman on the left is playing a harpsichord (similar to a piano).

It has a painted lid, which is propped open.

Jump to this page **or** follow the pipes.

Why? The oddest thing snatched in the Gardner Museum theft—a bronze-eagle flagpole topper valued at less than $100.

Isabella Stewart Gardner bought *The Concert* in a 1892 auction for $6,000.

Bathroom Break

Ah, dry land at last! Before we get to other matters, here's the second part of the page 47 puzzle.

iPuzzle

Concert-tration

Important! If you haven't read the puzzle instructions on page 47— do that now before reading the questions below.

1. How many people are in the painting? ______

2. How many people are standing?______

3. What hangs on the walls (including how many)?

____

4. What color is the floor? ________________________

5. What sort of item lies on the floor at the bottom of the painting (in the shadow)?________________________

6. From which direction is the light coming? ______________

7. How many people are wearing large purple hats?______

8. Is the head of the woman on the right tilted forward or backward?

____

Ms. Tirrius

As promised on page 3, here's a little bit about our invisible neighbor, Ms. Tirrius.

Nobody knows when Ms. Tirrius was born, or where. She doesn't even know herself…but then, she was only a little baby at the time.

Ms. Tirrius lives alone in a house next door to iFlush Labs. It used to be haunted, but the ghosts were too freaked out when she moved in, so they left and now haunt the nearby woods.

Ms. Tirrius's first name is unknown. She took a liking to the name Della a few years back and figured friends could call her that. But—she has no friends, so everyone just calls her Ms. Tirrius. (I'm sort of a friend, but I feel too small to call humans by their first names…even made-up ones.)

Ms. Tirrius wasn't always invisible. It happened in her younger years as a magician's assistant. One day, while doing a vanishing act…well, things went a little haywire. That's all she'll tell me.

Jump to this page **or** follow the pipes.

1896 **Where:** California's capital, Sacramento

High Lights

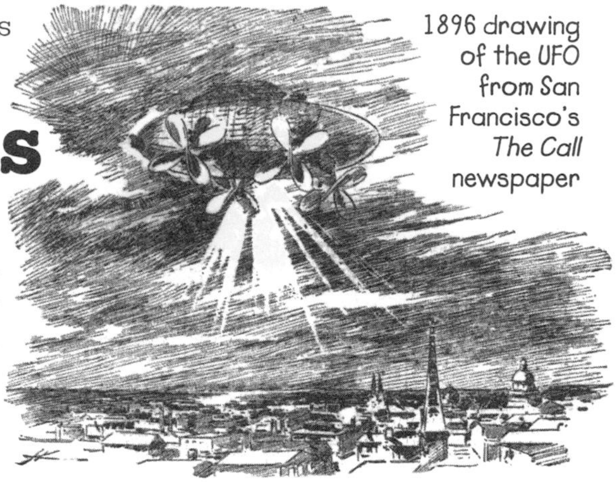

1896 drawing of the UFO from San Francisco's *The Call* newspaper

R. L. Lowery, a former railway worker, stares up at the night sky. He's spotted a bright light moving overhead. It's attached to an egg-shaped ship with fanlike wheels. More than a thousand other people see the light as well.

In the weeks to come, the **UFO** (unidentified flying object) would be seen as far north as **Canada** and 1,275 miles (2,000 km) south of that in **Los Angeles**.

Could it be a hot-air balloon? The first manned hot-air flight was in 1783, but this UFO was powered to fly into the wind. An airship? **Count Zeppelin** would make big news four years from now by flying a hydrogen-filled airship less than four miles (6 km). An airplane? The **Wright brothers** didn't make their first flight until 1903.

A lawyer named **George D. Collins** soon stepped forward. He claimed to represent a shy millionaire who had invented the airship people were seeing. But when no inventor appeared, the lawyer disappeared.

Things died down for several months, then in early 1897, the UFO sightings started up again. People saw it in Nebraska, then Kansas, Iowa, Texas, Missouri, and Illinois. Chicago **astronomers** tried to convince people they were seeing the planet **Venus**. But UFO spotters armed with telescopes believed otherwise, some claiming to hear voices coming from it.

Hoaxes followed—kids sent up lighted kites—and one Missouri man said he'd met a beautiful golden-haired woman from the UFO. But by April, the sightings stopped, and newspapers moved on to other stories. So what did all those people see? Your guess is as good as mine.

In April 1897, a Kansas farmer claimed a UFO airship stole one of his cows.

iPuzzle

Look! Up in the Sky!

Transfer the letters to the boxes to find nine common things people mistake for UFOs. Some of the letters aren't numbered, so you'll have to figure out where those go on your own.

13		11	9			3	1		12		17	2		7		16		5
P (crossed out)	L	A	N	T		P	E	E	L		E	X	A	M	I	N	E	R

1	2	3	4	5	6	7	8	9	10	11	12	■	13	14	15	16	17
												■	P				

5		10		12	1			14		7		4		8	
H	A	L	L	O	W	E	E	N		R	A	T		B.	O.

1	2	3	4	5	6	7	■	8	9	10	11	12	13	14

	7		13	5	9		10			1			8	11		2
E	N	E	R	G	Y	-	F	R	E	E			C	L	A	M

1	2	3	4	5	6	7	8	9	■	10	11	12	13	14

10	7		4	16		13		15	3			12	1		5		
A	R	T	I	F	I	C	I	A	L		A	R	M		T	R	Y

1	2	3	4	5	6	7	8	■	10	11	12	13	14	15	16	17

6		3	8	5			1	9	
L	I	T	T	L	E		S	E	A

1	2	3	4	5	6	7	8	9

	7			4		1	
O	N	E		M	O	T	H

1	2	3	■	4	5	6	7

5	12	9		6		4			1		8	11			14	15
D	I	M		F	O	U	L		C	A	R	T	O	O	N	S

1	2	3	4	5	■	6	7	8	9	10	11	12	13	14	15

3	10			8	11		4			14	1		5		7
T	E	R	R	I	B	L	E		E	L	M		O	A	F

1	2	3	4	5	6	■	7	8	9	10	11	12	13	14

12		2	11			1	7		8				5	
S	O	L	D		O	F	F		B	R	I	C	K	S

1	2	3	4	5	■	6	7	■	8	9	10	11	12

Every letter in each phrase will be used to fill the boxes.

Jump to this page **or** follow the pipes.

The Outlaws of the Air, an 1895 novel by George Griffith, is about a band of airship pirates.

1996

Where: A cave at the base of Mount Baigong, a cone-shaped hill in the center of China

Baigong Pipes

There's not much around here, just flat plains of red dirt and rock broken up by some shallow lakes and bare hills. Despite that, author **Bai Yu** has found something really interesting—a small triangular cave with what appear to be ancient metal pipes inside. More pieces of pipe lie along the shore of a nearby saltwater lake.

Bai Yu took a piece of pipe to a local metal-making plant for analysis. The engineer, **Liu Shaolin**, found it contained 30 percent iron oxide (rust), 62 percent silica and lime, and 8 percent unknown materials. "The pipes must be very old," Shaolin concluded. Bai Yu had just one thought—aliens.

In 2001 a team of Chinese **geologists** visited the cave to perform further tests. Their results showed the pipes to be about 150,000 years old, long before humans lived here. It must have been aliens!

Word quickly spread, and soon local artists put up a huge sandcastle-like monument along a nearby highway. The characters carved into one side read "Alien Ruins."

Were the pipes really an alien plumbing project? Cool as that would be, Chinese scientists eventually came up with a more likely, if no less weird, explanation—trees. During flooding, metal deposits would settle around tree roots. Then, when the trees died, rusty tubes would be left behind in the ground. Ta da—metal pipes!

Some people describe the area around Mount Baigong as looking more like Mars than Earth.

The Baigong Pipes range in size from needle-thin to 16 inches (40 cm) in diameter.

iPuzzle
Pipe Up
Find a way through the pipes from START to END.
End
Start

OOPart: That's short for "out of place artifact," a term used for items dating to a time when humans weren't capable of making them, such as the Baigong Pipes.

Year:
1997
Page:
40
Go
Return

Jump to this page **or** follow the pipes.

Baigong means "hill" in Chinese.

Pipes nearly identical to the Baigong Pipes have been found in the sandstone of the U.S. Southwest.

1990 **Where:** The courtyard inside CIA headquarters in Langley, Virginia

Hidden Meaning

Jim Sanborn, an artist, has stumped the **CIA**'s best spies and codebreakers. How? By creating a puzzling sculpture outside their offices he calls ***Kryptos***.

Kryptos is an S-shaped copper screen with 865 letters and four question marks cut out of it. Several rocks, a petrified log, and a small circular pool sit next to it. The left half of the copper screen contains a series of four coded messages that Sanborn and a retired CIA code expert, **Ed Scheidt**, dreamed up. The right half is a key for decoding those messages.

Sanborn figured it would take only a few weeks for the brains at the CIA to solve his puzzle. It took years! And that was just to crack the first three messages. The fourth is still unsolved.

In 1999 **Jim Gillogly**, a computer scientist from California, became the first person to announce he'd decoded the first three messages. Once he did, the CIA revealed that one of its analysts, **David Stein**, had solved those three parts a year earlier. Not to be outdone, the **NSA** (National Security Agency) said its own four-person team had done likewise back in 1992. (Documents released years later proved both claims.) But none of them could crack the fourth message.

So what does that pesky fourth part, just 97 letters long, say? Solvers around the world continue to work away, including a **yahoo.com** group of over 2,800 members.

The Decoded Solution... So Far

Part 1 of *Kryptos* reads: BETWEEN SUBTLE SHADING AND THE ABSENCE OF LIGHT LIES THE NUANCE OF IQLUSION.* Makes perfect sense, right? :-) Part 2 mentions a location 150 feet southwest of the sculpture, and part 3 is part of a quote about the opening of King Tut's tomb in 1922.

*Sanborn purposely omitted a letter in *Kryptos* and included some misspellings, including IQLUSION.

Kryptos means "hidden" in Greek.

iPuzzle

Spy Jokes

Use the key to decode the answer to each joke.

KEY

A	B	C	D	E	G	I	L	N	O	P	R	S	T	U	V
F	Q	2	J	4	M	H	1	Y	6	X	K	3	W	Z	5

1. What kind of spies hang out in department stores?

C ___ ___ ___ ___ ___ ___
2 6 Z Y W 4 K

___ ___ ___ ___ ___
3 X H 4 3

2. What do spies and gardeners have in common?

___ ___ ___ ___ ___ ___ and ___ ___ ___ ___
X 1 F Y W 3   Q Z M 3

3. What kind of spies sleep the most?

___ ___ ___ ___ ___ ___ ___ ___ ___ ___
Z Y J 4 K 2 6 5 4 K

___ ___ ___ ___ ___ ___
F M 4 Y W 3

This one works a little better written than spoken.

4. What's the difference between a SPECIAL AGENT and a CIA AGENT?

___, ___, ___, and ___
3 X 4 1

Jump to this page **or** follow the pipes.

In 2010 Sanborn revealed that NYPVTT decoded to BERLIN in the still-unsolved part of *Kryptos*.

1952 **Where:** The writing dens of five mystery book authors in the United States

Super Sleuths

There are lots of fun mystery-book series for kids. Best of all are the ones that mention my favorite animals—**rodents**!

A Rat! In a 1952 book, ***Mystery at the Ski Jump***, when **Nancy Drew** is handed a small mink, she accidentally drops it. The Drews' housekeeper, Hannah, sees the critter and jumps on a chair screaming, "A rat!" *Hmmph*, like there's something wrong with that! (BTW, Hannah, minks aren't even rodents.)

Loser! In a 1985 book, ***Nate the Great and the Fishy Prize***, a boy named Finley enters his rat named Rat in a Smartest Pet Contest. Despite some iffy competition—a pig, a parrot, an eel, four cats, and Nate's dog, Sludge—Rat doesn't win. :-(

Hiss! In a 1997 book, ***Cam Jansen and the Scary Snake Mystery***, a man blames Scaly the snake for eating his cream cheese sandwich. When a woman points out that Scaly only eats **live mice**, a bystander says, "That's digusting!" I second that.

Say Cheese! In a 1998 book, ***Encyclopedia Brown and the Case of the Sleeping Dog***, Encyclopedia attends a beauty show for mice. Maisie, a mouse owned by a girl named Maisie, takes first place and a cash prize of 50 cents. Hey, don't spend it all in one place, Maisie (either one). :-)

Lost! In another 1998 book, ***The Case of Hermie the Missing Hamster***, a boy named Wingnut loses one of his hamsters. Did it escape? Did his brother's snake eat it? Luckily, **Jigsaw Jones** and his partner Mila are on Hermie's trail . . . for a dollar a day.

The letters in NATE THE GREAT can be rearranged to spell THAT TEENAGER or THEATER AGENT.

. . . Nancy Drew books inspired both Hillary Clinton and Laura Bush when they were kids.

iPuzzle

Whodunit?

Someone stole Dwayne's cheese. Use the clues to nail the thief.

The cheese burglar...

... doesn't hang out in a sty
... never smiles
... isn't wearing a hat
... doesn't have a mustache
... doesn't eat hay
... doesn't have a beard
... doesn't take tongue baths
... doesn't wear glasses
... doesn't like purple
... doesn't have a name tag
... isn't bald
... is?

Jump to this page **or** follow the pipes.

Encyclopedia Brown starred in his own comic strip from 1978 to 1980.

70 B.C. **Where:** At sea near the Greek isle of Antikythera

Island Time

About 1/4 actual size

Part of the recovered Antikythera mechanism

I've boarded a Roman ship headed for **Italy**. Treasures fill its hold—vases, bronze and marble sculptures, jewelry, and an incredibly complex Greek machine that will come to be known as the **Antikythera mechanism**.

My timing is a bit off, though. As soon as I find a comfy spot on deck, a storm crashes us into rocks along the coast of **Antikythera**. The ship and its treasures are sent to the bottom of the **Mediterranean Sea**. Luckily, my iSwirl whisks me away just in time...

...and fast-forwards me to the year 1900. A Greek **sponge diver** has just discovered the Roman shipwreck, untouched for 2,000 years. He and his pals bring up a few of the treasures. The following year, additional helpers will recover more of the valuable cargo. Each find is amazing, but the **Antikythera mechanism** is the real jaw-dropper. It's far more advanced than anything ever found from that time period.

The machine can plot the position of the sun and moon day by day as well as display the **moon's phase** (whether it's full, half, etc.). On the front, the days, months, and an **astrological calendar** are marked on a large dial. Inside is a complicated arrangement of 30 interlocking gears, equal in design to the finest Swiss watch. On the back are two more dials. One double-checks the mechanism's accuracy with a 19-year calendar. The other predicts solar and lunar **eclipses**. A small crank on the side makes it all work.

What the mechanism originally looked like

Who invented this incredible machine? What exactly was it used for? Just how advanced *were* the Greeks? Researchers continue to hunt for the answers.

Note: the iSwirl's accuracy on B.C. dates is not exact. This year could be a bit earlier...or later.

Some people call the Antikythera mechanism the world's first computer.

iPuzzle

Like Clockwork

To find the answer to joke #1, start at the red letter. Write that letter (L) in the first blank, followed by *every other letter*, traveling clockwise. Do the same for joke #2, but starting at the blue letter (I).

1. What sound does a clock make on the moon?

L ___ ___ ___-

___ ___ ___ ___

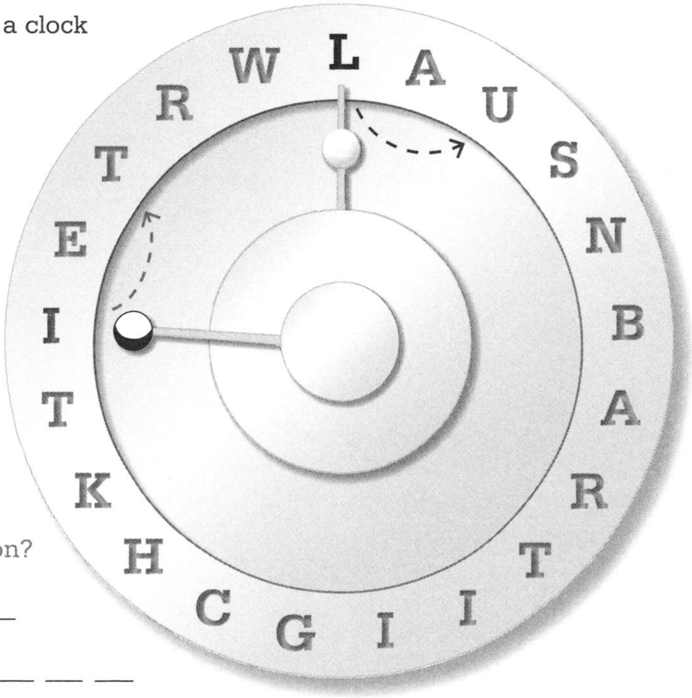

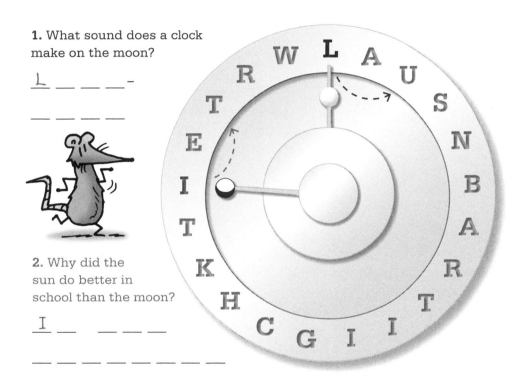

2. Why did the sun do better in school than the moon?

I ___ ___ ___ ___

___ ___ ___ ___ ___ ___ ___ ___

One Guess: Some people have suggested the great thinker Archimedes invented the Antikythera mechanism. He knew a lot about astronomy and engineering, and it's believed he wrote a paper about astronomical mechanisms that was lost long ago. Also, month names found etched into the mechanism match those used in the area where Archimedes lived.

Jump to this page **or** follow the pipes.

Anitkythera is pronounced "ann-tee-kith-ear-uh."

Solar eclipse: when the moon blocks the sun. *Lunar eclipse*: when Earth blocks sunlight to the moon.

1198 **Where:** Yorkshire, a large county in northern England

Human Beans

William of Newburgh, an English historian and monk, has just finished writing his ***History of English Affairs***. The title may sound highfalutin, but don't let it fool you. The book includes a really cool story about two green children. It happened around the middle of the twelfth century in **Woolpit, England**....

Woolpit is a sleepy village of about 100 peasants and a few lords. It sits in the shadow of a grand abbey just to the west. The town's name comes not from wool but from wolf pits dug in the nearby woods to rid the English countryside of the sharp-toothed beasts.

One day, at harvest time, a group of field workers discovered a young boy and girl near the wolf pits. The children wore odd clothes, spoke a language no one could understand, and strangest of all—their skin was green!

A man named Sir Richard de Caine took in the pea-headed pair. He tried to get them to eat, but they refused...until one day when they saw some beanstalks. They motioned to be given the beans, which they gobbled up. It was months before they ate anything else.

The boy soon died. But the girl got stronger and learned the villagers' language. She told them that she and her brother had come from a land where the sun never shone. They had been lured through a long cave by the sound of Woolpit's church bells. The girl's green color eventually faded away, and she lived out the rest of her years in Woolpit.

Is the tale true? William reported it as if it were, and people have been telling it for hundreds of years. The town even has a sign with the green children on it. →

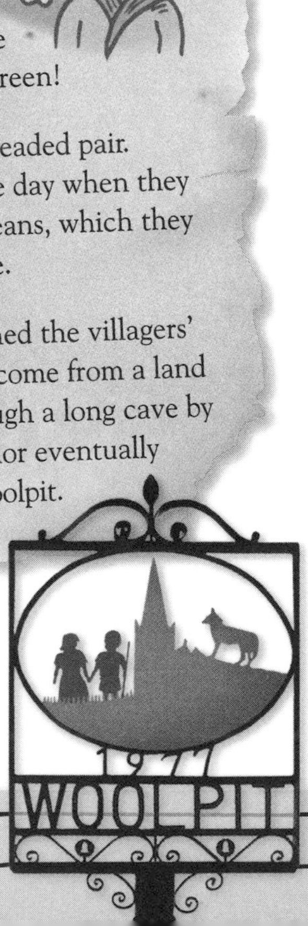

...Arsenic poisoning and a type of anemia caused by low iron can cause a greenish tinge to the skin.

...Green added to red on a computer screen produces yellow.

iPuzzle

Greenery

Each shade of green in the box is spelled out in one of the sentences below. The letters are split between at least two words, as shown in the example.

FERN	HUNTER	LIME	MOSS	PEA
FOREST	KELLY	MINT	~~OLIVE~~	SHAMROCK

1. THE GREEN CHILDREN NEEDED BEANS T[O LIVE].
2. I HOPE A GREEN DRAGON NEVER COMES NEAR ME.
3. HAVING A GREEN THUMB GAVE HIM A SLIM EDGE.
4. ATTILA THE HUN TERRIFIED THE GREEN BERETS.
5. THE ESKIMOS SAILED TO GREENLAND.
6. WE OFFER NO GREEN CHEESE HERE.
7. I SAW A SILVER NICKEL LYING ON A GREEN PICKLE.
8. HE TOOK A VITAMIN TABLET WITH HIS GREEN SALAD.
9. MY GREEN EGGS, COMBINED WITH HIS HAM, ROCKED!
10. HE USED A NET FOR ESTIMATING THE GREEN TURTLE'S WEIGHT.

iPuzzle Quickie

Match up the jokes and punch lines.

1. ___ What did the lettuce say to the celery?

2. ___ What's the strongest vegetable?

3. ___ What's the angriest vegetable?

A. Grump-pea.

B. Quit stalking me.

C. A muscle sprout.

Jump to this page **or** follow the pipes.

In ancient China and Japan, one character stood for both green and blue: 青.

1914

Where: Brooklyn, New York, the home of Sam Loyd...

Puzzle King

What are **puzzles**? They're man-made mysteries. And just like the real mysteries life throws at us, puzzles can cause a lot of head scratching and muttering. But there's one big difference—puzzles always have an answer. That's what makes them so much fun.

Sam Loyd thought puzzles were fun...and a good way to make a living. Some people call him the world's greatest puzzle maker ever. He wrote puzzles, collected puzzles, published puzzles, and sometimes even claimed credit for other people's puzzles. And now, three years after his death, Sam Loyd's son, Walther, finally put all that work into one big book.

Loyd's first love was **chess**. As a teenager, he won prizes for chess problems he dreamed up (chessboard arrangements with clever solutions). In 1855 when Sam was 14, the ***New York Saturday Courier*** printed one of them.

As an adult, Loyd shifted to puzzles. He edited ***Sam Loyd's Puzzle Magazine*** and produced popular cardboard puzzles. His "**Get Off the Earth**" puzzle, with two rotating disks that changed 13 people into 12, sold 10 million copies. Or so Loyd said. He made all sorts of claims, true or not.

For example, in 1896 Loyd reminded readers how he "drove the entire world crazy with a little box of movable blocks." The **14-15 puzzle** he referred to required solvers to reverse the numbers 14 and 15 by shifting one block at a time. Just one problem—Loyd had nothing to do with it. **Noyes Chapman**, a postmaster, had invented the novelty. And in 1879 **Matthias Rice** sold it as **The Gem Puzzle**, creating a national craze. Still, in true Sam Loyd style, the "puzzle king" offered a prize of $1,000 for a correct solution. Loyd's money was safe. It had been proven long before that the puzzle was impossible.

...Sam Loyd once sold a "Trick Mules" puzzle for $10,000 to P. T. Barnum to use as a giveaway at his circus.

The 14-15 puzzle was so popular in 1880, employers banned it from the workplace during office hours.

iPuzzle

How Puzzling

Here are two puzzles from Sam Loyd's 1914 book.

1. Find a route through the Martian canals that visits each letter once and only once. The correct route will spell out a sentence. Many people have claimed: "There is no possible way." But it can be solved.

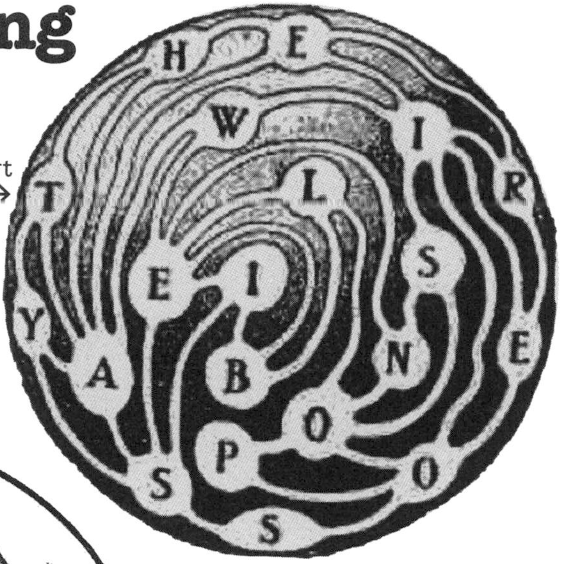

2. Below are the 10 numbers displayed on the dolls in the drawing. Which combination of dolls must be knocked down to equal exactly 50?

(25) (27)

(3) (12) (6)

(15) (9) (30) (21) (19)

Watch Compass: Here's a handy tip from Sam Loyd on how to use your watch as a compass. Hold your watch parallel to the ground with the hour hand pointing at the sun. The halfway mark between the hour hand and 12 will be south (north if you live south of the equator.)

Jump to this page **or** follow the pipes.

As a child, Sam Loyd practiced ventriloquism around his home, fooling the hired help.

950 B.C. **Where:** I promised not to say...but it *might* be London, Yale University, and the Netherlands

"What's the Password?"

Have you ever created a **secret clubhouse**? No boys (or no girls) allowed. It seems some people never outgrow that urge. Here are three super-secret organizations created by grown-ups.

The Freemasons trace their roots to **King Solomon** and the workers who built the **Temple in Jerusalem** around 950 B.C. By the year 1717 the Freemasons had grown into an organization of men looking to improve themselves and the world. Members met in lodges using a secret handshake and password. According to an oath they took, the penalty for revealing any of this insider stuff was...death! Several of America's founding fathers were Freemasons, including **George Washington** and **Benjamin Franklin**. Many people think that explains the pyramid and triangular eye on the back of the $1 bill, considered to be Freemason symbols.

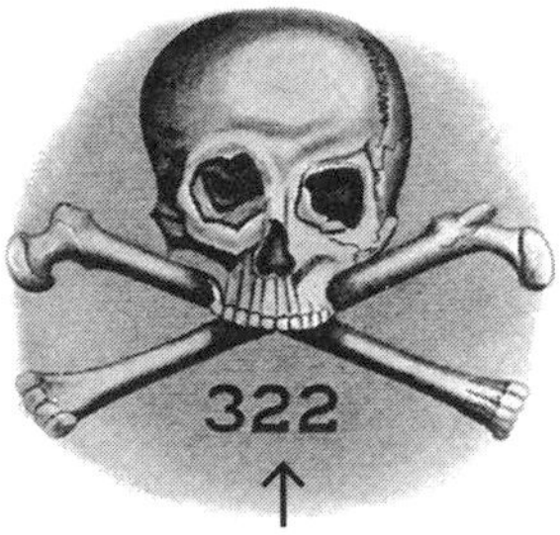

The meaning of this number is uncertain.

Skull and Bones was formed at **Yale University** in 1832. Each year, a new crop of 15 seniors is added. Members, known as Bonesmen, meet twice a week in the **Tomb**, a windowless campus building, to discuss...well, only they know. Supposedly, hanging inside the Tomb are the stolen skulls of **Geronimo**, the Apache chief, and **Pancho Villa**, the Mexican revolutionary.

The Bilderberg Group is an annual meeting of world, military, and business leaders, first held in 1954 at the **Hotel de Bilderberg** in **Oosterbeek, Netherlands**. Do they talk about world domination? That's what some people think. But only those with invitations get inside the armed checkpoints... so what's said at Bilderberg, stays at Bilderberg!

iPuzzle

Rat Latin

Would you like to join the Rat Club? All you have to do is learn Rat Latin, our secret way of writing and talking.

Here's how it works:

1. Locate the first vowel in a word.
2. Insert AT before that vowel.

For example, HELLO would be HATELLO and RAT LATIN would be RATAT LATATIN.

Okay, let's practice.
First, decode these Rat Latin sentences:

WATELCOME TATO TATHE CLATUB: ______

DATO YATOU LATIKE LATIMBURGER? ______

Now convert these sentences to Rat Latin:

I LIKE YOUR TAIL: ______

DWAYNE IS THE BEST: ______

COULD YOU SQUEAK UP? ______

I LIVE ON A FARM: ______

EXTRA CREDIT: Add AT *twice* to each set of letters to form a common phrase.

1. F C: FAT CAT

2. BH M: ______

3. ME & POTOES: ______

4. WEHER STION: ______

Jump to this page **or** follow the pipes.

1904 **Where:** Berlin, Germany, with an astounding horse

Horse Sense

Hans and teacher

Hans has got to be the smartest horse in the world. He can understand and read German, solve math problems, tell time, identify people in photos, and use a kind of sign language by stomping his right hoof or moving his head.

A retired math teacher, **Wilhelm von Osten**, trained Hans to do all those things. For example, he'd show Hans three **wooden pins** and say the word "three." When the stallion stomped his hoof three times, he'd get a lump of sugar or a piece of bread. That taught Hans numbers and words, both at the same time. He soon moved on to addition, subtraction, division, multiplication, and many other brainy feats.

Clever Hans, as he came to be known, began showing off his skills in a courtyard outside his stall. Many amazed onlookers suspected the act was a trick, but how? The **Berlin Board of Education** decided to find out. They appointed a 13-person panel that included a psychologist, a circus manager, a vet, and the director of the Berlin Zoo. They watched the horse closely but could find no trickery!

Clever Hans performs.

The panel decided to set up a tent to conduct experiments. The tests were particularly telling. Clever Hans answered correctly almost every time when von Osten or another questioner knew the answer, but almost never when they didn't!

As it turned out, Clever Hans was no math genius. But he was a genius of another sort—being able to notice the slightest reactions his questioners made when, for example, Hans stomped his foot the correct number of times. The humans' cues were so small, a slight nod or relaxing of a muscle, they didn't even realize they were making them!

Giving answers based on a questioner's body language came to be known as the Clever Hans Effect.

iPuzzle

Whinny Ha-Ha

Match up each horse joke with the correct punch line.

1. ___ Why did the pony have to gargle?
2. ___ What's the difference between a bronco and a tame horse?
3. ___ Why did the farmer ride his horse to town?
4. ___ What did the horse say when it fell down?
5. ___ What do you ask a sad horse?
6. ___ What kind of horses like the dark best?
7. ___ What's the difference between a horse and a duck?
8. ___ Why did the horse eat with its mouth open?
9. ___ What do you get if you cross a horse with a wild pig?
10. ___ What kind of bread does a racehorse like best?

A. Nightmares.
B. About 20 bucks.
C. A neigh boar.
D. It was too heavy to carry.
E. Thoroughbred.
F. Bad stable manners.
G. It was a little ho(a)rse.
H. "Why the long face?"
I. One goes quick, the other goes quack.
J. "I can't giddyup."

Speak! In 1930 a German woman named Margarethe Schmidt founded Hundesprechschule Asra, a school with the goal of teaching dogs how to talk. The government encouraged her work, hoping to use the dogs against its enemies. Alas, Schmidt was barking up the wrong tree. Her hounds all flunked out, and the school shut down in 1945.

Jump to this page **or** follow the pipes.

In 1916, Clever Hans was taken for use in World War II, never to be heard of again.

1937 **Where:** North Salem, New Hampshire, home to an ancient archaeological site…or just a weird pile of rocks

Stones in the Sticks

Welcome to **Mystery Hill**. A retired insurance executive named **William Goodwin** has just bought this 30-acre plot. He calls it "the most amazing ruins of a stone village…I have ever seen." The site features chambers made of hand-cut rock, a four-and-a-half-ton granite table with a groove carved around its edge, and notched stones jutting out of the earth.

At first, Goodwin suspected he'd discovered **Vinland**, a long-lost Viking village. When that didn't add up, he convinced himself that **Irish monks** had created Mystery Hill more than 100 years before **Columbus** arrived in America.

Based on that theory, Goodwin began reconstructing a monk village. Workers dug up some of the stones and moved others using teams of oxen. Unfortunately, when nobody else bought the monk idea, it was too late—Goodwin had forever ruined the ruins. From that point on, it was anybody's guess as to how things had originally looked.

Later studies produced a mixed bag of ideas. Charcoal pits on the site were found to be up to 4,000 years old. Had some ancient civilization built Mystery Hill…or were the ashes just leftovers from earlier times? A vein of **quartz crystal** discovered at the bottom of a well raised a few eyebrows. Some Old World civilizations had used crystals in their religious ceremonies. Also, the placement of stones seemed to track the sun's position, suggesting an **astronomical calendar** to some.

Others shrugged off these ideas as "crackpot," viewing the site as nothing more than some walls and sheds built by American Indians or colonists.

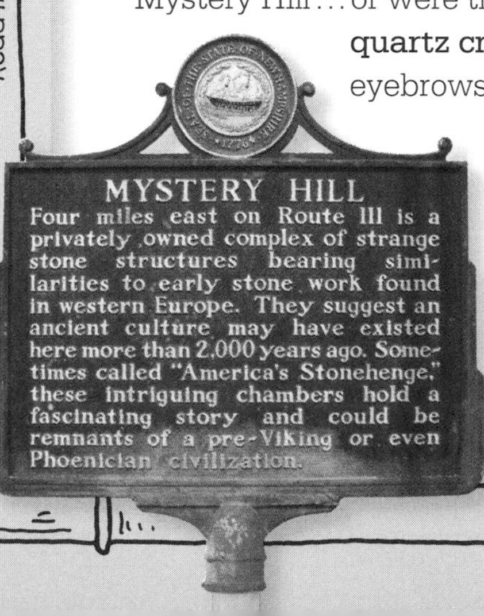

MYSTERY HILL
Four miles east on Route 111 is a privately owned complex of strange stone structures bearing similarities to early stone work found in western Europe. They suggest an ancient culture may have existed here more than 2,000 years ago. Sometimes called "America's Stonehenge," these intriguing chambers hold a fascinating story and could be remnants of a pre-Viking or even Phoenician civilization.

Read more about the Viking's Vinland in *iFlush: Hurtling thru History*, page 42.

No ancient relics (pottery, tools) have ever been found at Mystery H

iPuzzle

Stone Work

Draw in the 10 blocks (or just write in the numbers) so that they read MYSTERY HILL, followed by an arrow pointing to the right.

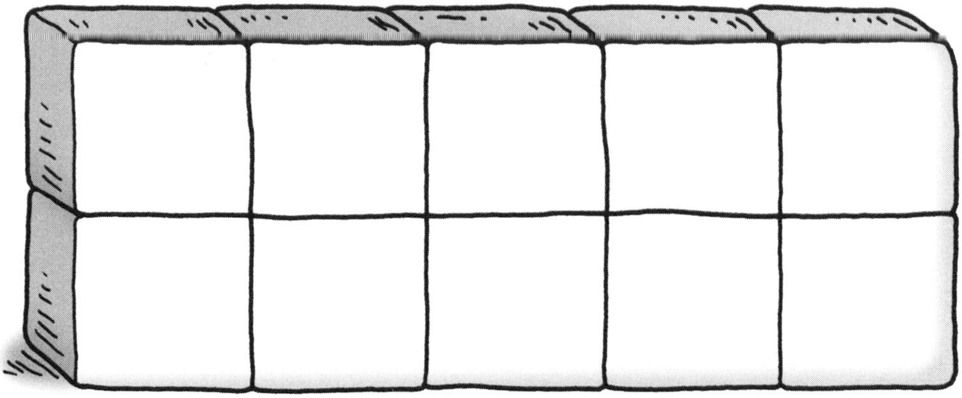

Jump to this page **or** follow the pipes.

In 1982 Mystery Hill was renamed America's Stonehenge, a paid-admission tourist attraction.

1812 **Where:** The port of Georgetown, South Carolina, watching a ship named the *Patriot* head out to sea on New Year's Eve

Waves Goodbye

Art from the *San Francisco Call*, 1906

I set the **iSwirl** for mid-afternoon, when the *Patriot* was scheduled to leave. But it shoved off early. I missed the boat! Maybe that's just as well, since none of its passengers will survive the voyage—including **Theodosia Burr Alston**, daughter of former vice president **Aaron Burr**.

What happened? Nobody really knows, but there's one possibility I like because it involves...pirates!

The hold of the *Patriot* was filled with treasure, having just returned from raiding British ships in the **Caribbean** (the **War of 1812** was in full swing). For this trip—a mission to deliver that booty, barrels of rice, and Ms. Alston to **New York**—the captain disguised the ship. He painted over its name on the bow and stowed its cannons below.

He hoped that might fool the British if they stopped the ship. But it also meant the *Patriot* would be unprotected if pirates attacked—and that's just what happened. According to the deathbed confessions of two men, one unnamed fellow in 1933 and **"Old Frank" Burdick** in 1848, each of them was among a band of looters that killed the *Patriot* crew, took their valuables, and then made Alston walk the plank. The young woman faced it bravely, Burdick said, asking only that her father and husband be told of her fate. They weren't.

Of course, some people think the *Patriot* might have just gone down in a violent storm, but—yawn—how boring is that?

She Was Framed!

"Old Frank" Burdick said he saw a painting of Theodosia Alston on the *Patriot*. In 1869 Dr. William Pool found what *might* be the same painting (next page) in Nags Head, North Carolina, supposedly recovered from an 1813 shipwreck.

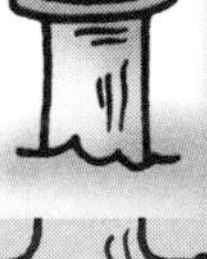

Vice President Aaron Burr killed a political opponent, Alexander Hamilton, in an 1804 duel.

iPuzzle

Something's Different

What one thing in each portrait is different from the original?

original

1. ________________

2. ________________

3. ________________

4. ________________

5. ________________

6. ________________

7. ________________

8. ________________

9. ________________

10. ________________

Jump to this page **or** follow the pipes.

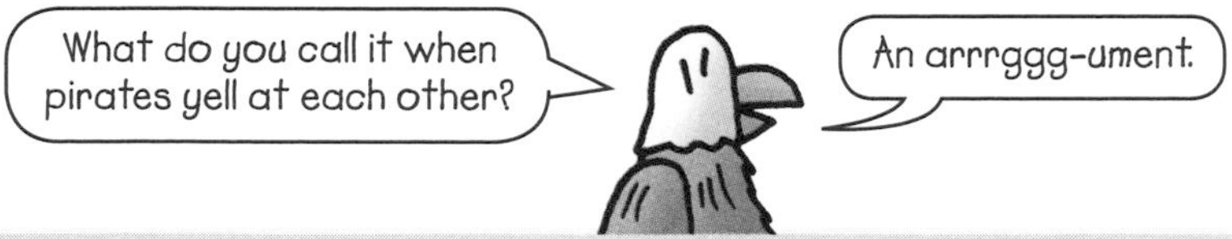

What do you call it when pirates yell at each other?
An arrrggg-ument.

In 1802 Theodosia and Joseph Alston honeymooned at Niagara Falls, the first recorded couple to do so.

1941

Where: A dry plain in Peru between the towns of Nazca and Palpas

It's a "Dirty" Job

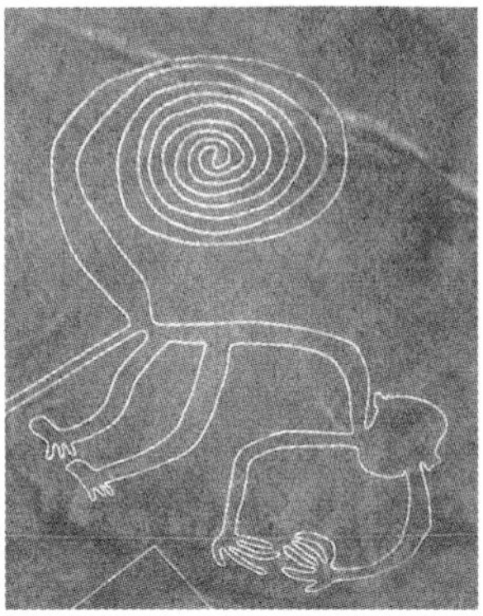
The Nazca monkey

Imagine a **monkey** the size of a football field. Or a **condor** that's taller than the **Statue of Liberty**. Both those creatures can be found here in **Peru**, flat on the ground. No, they're not some oversized roadkill— they're ancient drawings that the **Nazca people** carved into the dirt about 1,500 years ago.

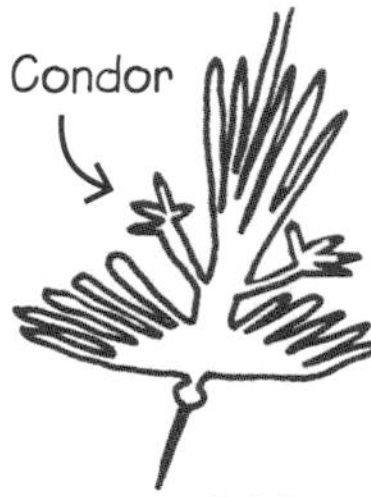

Why? That's what **Maria Reiche** is here to find out. She's not the first person to study these **geoglyphs**, known as the **Nazca Lines**, but she's certainly the most dedicated. She'll spend more than 50 years staring at the ground around here.

Hundreds of triangles, rectangles, and long straight lines decorate this desert landscape. Even cooler are the spirals, zigzags, plant shapes, and about three dozen animals, including a dog, a spider, and a hummingbird.

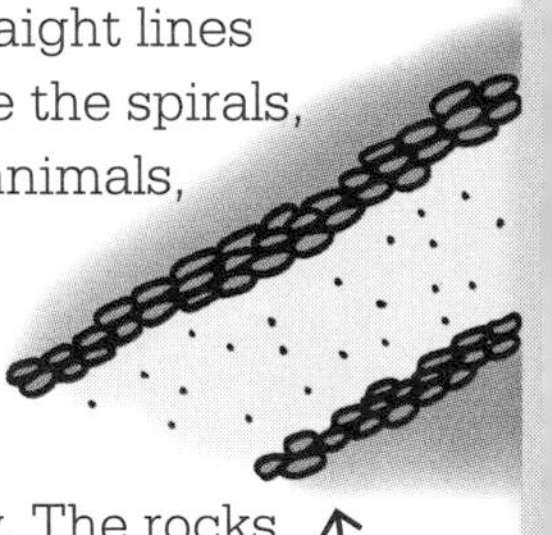

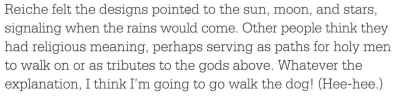

To make the lines, or paths, really, workers removed a 12-inch layer (30 cm) of rust-colored rocks to reveal the yellowish-white sand below. The rocks were then stacked on either side of the lines as a border.

Reiche felt the designs pointed to the sun, moon, and stars, signaling when the rains would come. Other people think they had religious meaning, perhaps serving as paths for holy men to walk on or as tributes to the gods above. Whatever the explanation, I think I'm going to go walk the dog! (Hee-hee.)

Nine Fingers

In the early 1930s, Maria Reiche lost a finger due to a bad infection. Years later, when she saw the giant Nazca monkey—with a total of nine fingers on its two hands—she knew this was the place for her!

The Nazca Lines vary in width from one to 10 feet (.3 to 3 meters).

Maria Reiche was nicknamed the Lady of the Lines.

iPuzzle

What's Dot?

Connect the dots to reveal the drawing we made in the dirt outside iFlush Labs.

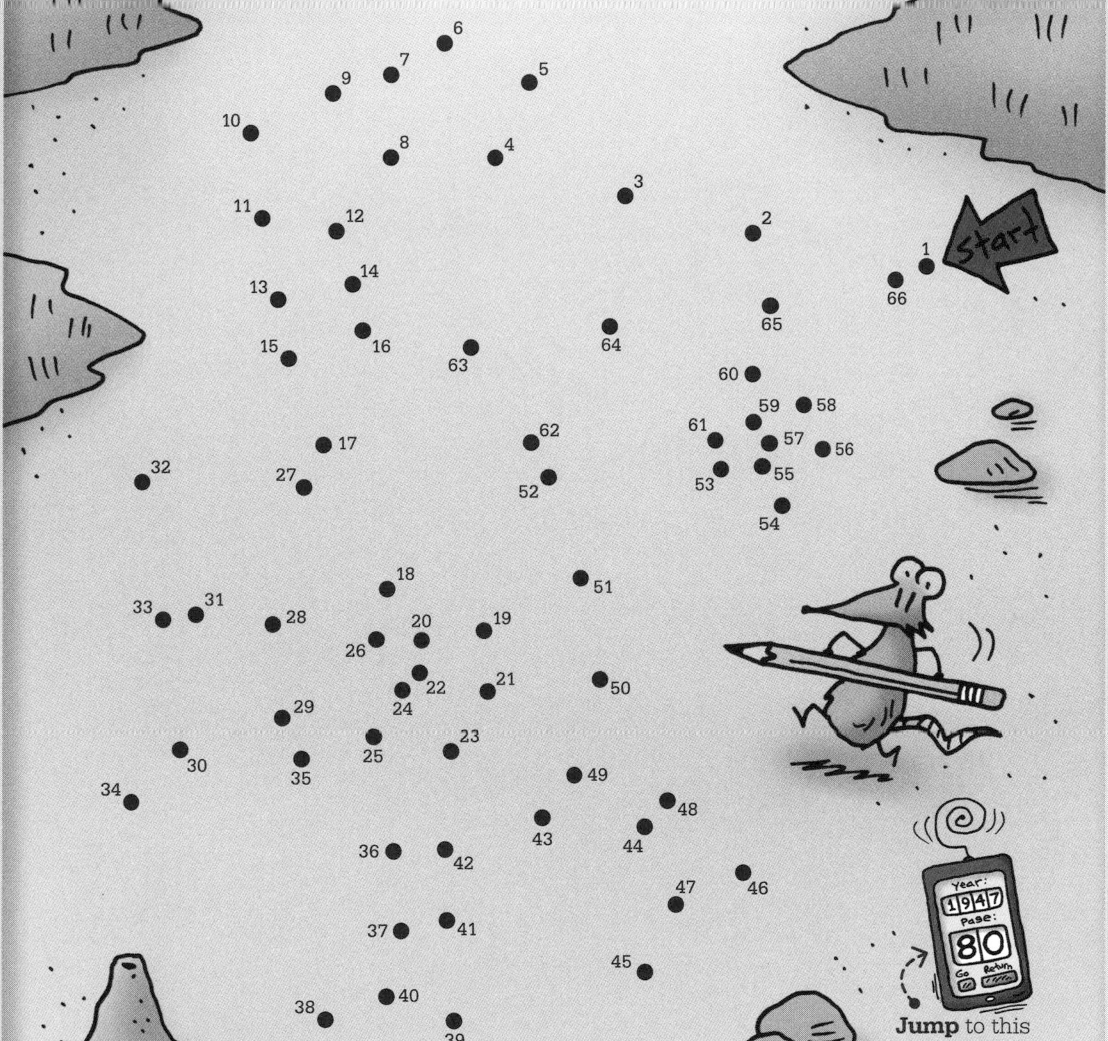

Jump to this page **or** follow the pipes.

1885 **Where:** Standing outside a print shop in Lynchburg, Virginia, to get the first copy of a 24-page pamphlet, *The Beale Papers*

Buried Treasure

Gold, silver, jewels! According to this pamphlet, that's what **Thomas J. Beale** buried not far from here about 65 years ago. If the treasure exists, it would be worth millions!

What's the story? I took notes as I leafed through ***The Beale Papers***:

In 1817 Thomas J. Beale and about 30 pals went to New Mexico to hunt buffalo and grizzly bears.

They ended up discovering gold and silver instead!

The group hauled the treasure to Virginia and buried it near Buford's Tavern.

In 1822 Beale wrote three coded pages that described the treasure, where it was buried, and how it should be divided up. He put the pages in a locked iron box, along with two regularly written notes, and gave the box to Robert Morriss.

Morriss was told only that it contained valuable papers and that he should open it in 10 years if he heard nothing further.

Ten years passed with no word from Beale. Then 13 more. Finally, in 1845, Morriss broke open the box.

He read Beale's notes, which explained that the three coded pages would reveal everything about the treasure. Just one problem. A decoding key that Morriss should have received in 1832 had never come!

In 1862, after years of trying to decode the pages, Morriss shared them with an unnamed friend. That friend decoded one page (it described the treasure's content), but got nowhere with the other two. In 1885 Morriss's friend decided to print *The Beale Papers* so others could try.

Here's what that decoded page reveals: 2,912 pounds of **gold** (1,320 kg), 5,100 pounds of **silver** (2,313 kg), and $13,000 worth of **jewels** were buried in iron pots four miles from **Buford's Tavern**.

But is the pamphlet true? According to a 1982 article in *The Virginia Magazine of History and Biography* by **Joe Nickell**—no. Among other things in the story, he found incorrect dates and words unknown when it was supposedly written. Still, if you ever go near Buford's and see people digging, you'll know why.

Beale converted some of the gold and silver to jewels. They'd be worth about $195,000 in 2014.

In 2014 dollars, 2,912 pounds of gold would be worth about $60 million.

iPuzzle

Buried Letters

Below is the cover of *The Beale Papers*. Follow the instructions to "dig up" letters that will answer this joke:

What baseball equipment would be handy for keeping a treasure chest safe?

1 THE
2 BEALE PAPERS,
3 CONTAINING
4 AUTHENTIC STATEMENTS
5 REGARDING THE
6 TREASURE BURIED
7 IN
8 1819 AND 1821,
9 NEAR
10 BUFORDS, IN BEDFORD COUNTY, VIRGINIA
11 line 11, first word, first letter AND
12 WHICH HAS NEVER BEEN RECOVERED.
13 PRICE FIFTY CENTS
14 LYNCHBURG;
15 VIRGINIAN BOOK AND JOB PRINT,
16 1885

How to "dig up" letters below:
The first number in each series matches one of the red numbers on the pamphlet cover. The second number indicates which word to go to on that line. The third number indicates which letter to take from that word. We've found the first one for you.

A 11 • 1 • 1

___ 12 • 5 • 3
___ 1 • 1 • 2
___ 13 • 3 • 2
___ 4 • 2 • 1
___ 4 • 2 • 2

___ 2 • 2 • 1
___ 14 • 1 • 8
___ 3 • 1 • 2
___ 6 • 1 • 1
___ 10 • 3 • 2
___ 10 • 4 • 1
___ 5 • 2 • 1
___ 15 • 2 • 2
___ 9 • 1 • 4

Jump to this page **or** follow the pipes.

In 2014 dollars, 5,100 pounds of silver would be worth about $1.7 million.

2014 **Where:** Wandering the neighborhood around iFlush Labs . . . lurking and listening

Didya Ever Wonder?

I've been collecting everyday mysteries. Those nagging little thoughts that people wonder about, some puzzling, some weird, some just plain goofy. There seems to be no end to them. Maybe you've even had a few yourself.

If F stands for FAIL, what do A, B, C, and D stand for? And why is there no E?

After a building is finished, shouldn't it be called a built?

Why does Superman wear his underpants over his tights?

How come you never see fish sleeping on the bottom of the ocean?

If Americans throw rice at a wedding, do Japanese people throw french fries?

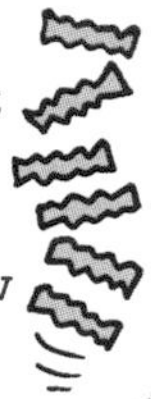

Why can't you buy cat-flavored dog food?

Why is the word MINIATURE much bigger than the word BIG?

If the days of the week all end in DAY, why don't the months all end in MONTH?

Why is your butt called your bottom when it's in the middle of your body?

How do you handcuff an octopus?

Where does the white go when snow melts?

Z Z Z Z Z

What if dreaming is real life, and being awake is a dream?

Why do people eat limburger cheese?

Why are there no letters next to 1 on a telephone keypad?

"What is the meaning of life?" is the most popular unanswerable question on ask.com. →

A penny for your thoughts

iPuzzle

Whadya Think?

Your two cents

Are there unanswered questions that keep you up at night…or daydreaming during history class?

There are no right answers here…just write questions.

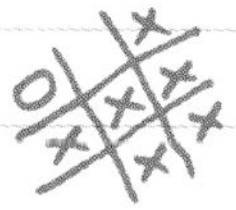

Here are a few categories to get you started:
movie theaters, lunch, Road Runner cartoons, gym class, parents, school, sport utility vehicles, politicians, cats.

Jump to this page **or** follow the pipes.

1782 **Where:** A limestone quarry in Passy, a suburb of Paris, France (in later years, part of Paris)

Toad-ally Awesome

The workers here have just made a startling discovery, something they've never seen at the quarry before. They cracked open four **limestone** rocks and found…a live **toad** inside each one!

When they told their boss, **Jacques-Donatien Le Ray de Chaumont**, he knew just the person to tell—his old pal **Benjamin Franklin**. Franklin, always the curious scientist, was serving as ambassador to France at the time. He lived just a stone's throw from the quarry and hustled over to check it out.

The workers showed Franklin two of the toads and described how they'd found them. Each was surrounded by a clump of moist yellowish soil in a hollow chunk of limestone rock. The rocks had no openings and were found 15 feet below the surface (4.5 m). Ancient seashells nearby suggested that the area had been untouched for thousands of years. Had these toads found a way to live forever?

It turns out these quarry workers aren't the only people in history to report such a discovery. In 1862 **Charles Dickens** (author of *A Christmas Carol*) wrote: "I have read stories about [frogs] being found alive in holes, in the centre of blocks of marble where they could not have found any entrance nor any air." And at London's **International Exhibition**, also in 1862, a frog was put on display next to the lump of coal it was supposedly found inside.

How can this be? Toads *do* have the ability to **hibernate** burrowed into the ground or underwater, and for up to three years. But for thousands of years inside a rock?

In 1825 English geologist **William Buckland** decided to conduct a test. He placed a dozen toads in hollowed-out limestone blocks. Many survived one year, but none lasted two. So, it's a puzzling situation, one that might require leaving no stone unturned.

Some limestone is very porous, able to let in a lot of water and air.

Ben Franklin could play the harp and was once president of Pennsylvania.

iPuzzle

Hop to It

Following the arrows from rock to rock, find the one path that will take this toad from START to END.

Raining Frogs: In 2009 people across Japan reported finding tadpoles, fish, and frogs covering the ground. Scientists think waterspouts might have sucked the critters up, then dropped them from the sky…but nobody is really sure.

Jump to this page **or** follow the pipes.

Both frogs and toads can croak, although not all species and only the males.

1947 **Where:** In a plane circling Mount Rainier in the state of Washington

What Was That?

It's 2:59 in the afternoon on June 24, and I'm sitting behind **Kenneth Arnold**, the pilot of this three-seater airplane. While traveling to the city of **Yakima**, Arnold decided to take a detour to look for a missing Marine airplane. It was last seen near **Mount Rainier**.

He hasn't been having any luck, but—wait, what's that? Arnold has spotted nine unusual aircraft about 20 miles away. They're lined up diagonally like geese in the sky, moving at a speed Arnold estimates to be 1,200 mph (1,931 kph). That's nearly twice the current airspeed record! And get this—the ships are mirror-bright and round. About three minutes later, the mysterious aircraft disappear from view, and Arnold continues on his way.

Newspapers latched on to the story soon after Arnold told others what he'd seen. Two days later, a headline in ***The Chicago Sun*** read: "Supersonic Flying Saucers Sighted by Idaho Pilot." It marked the first known use of the term "**flying saucer**."

That got the attention of both the **Army Air Force** (AAF) and the **FBI**. Was something up there they should know about? On July 9, they started looking into Arnold's claims as well as sightings others had reported. After interviewing Arnold, two AAF officers concluded, "Mr. Arnold actually saw what he stated he saw."

In 1948 the Air Force launched **Operation SIGN** to look into unidentified aircraft sightings. Soon renamed **Project Blue Book**, it lasted until 1969, when the military decided the program offered no scientific value.

As for what Arnold saw that day, we still don't know. "It is just as much a mystery to me as it is to the rest of the world," he said. "It seems impossible, but there it is."

From 1947 to 1949, the Air Force received reports of 12,618 unidentified aircraft sightings. →

iPuzzle

UFOdoku

saucer

sun

bird

cloud

Draw in the missing pictures following the rules in the example.

All 4 pictures in each column

All 4 pictures in each row

All 4 pictures in each bold box

1.

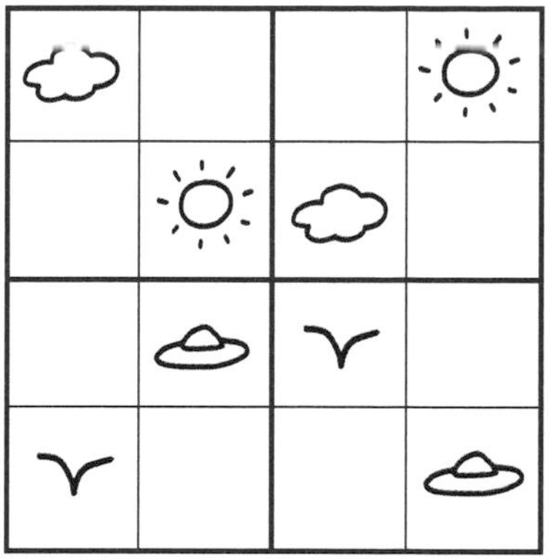

2.

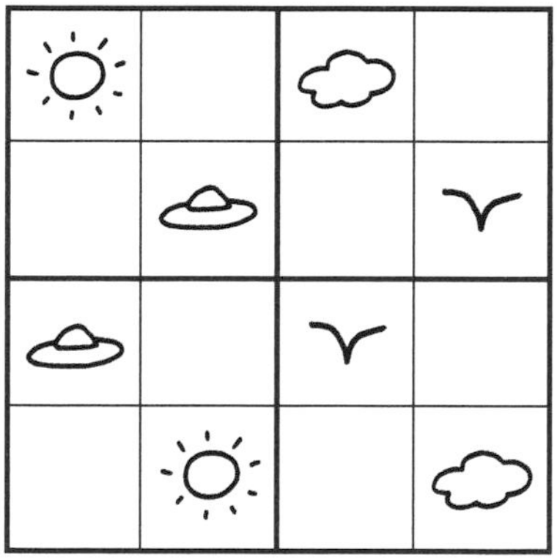

3.

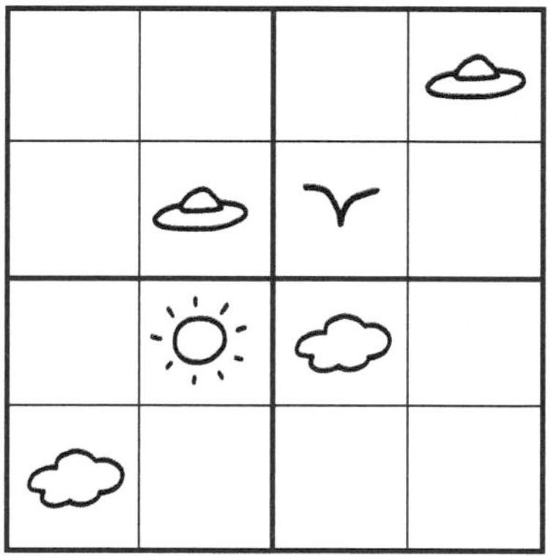

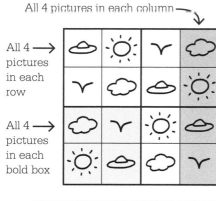

Roswell: In 1947 something crashed from the sky near Roswell, New Mexico. On July 8, an Army Air Force press release identified it as a "flying disc," but hours later a general stated it was merely a weather balloon. Ever since, people have accused the military of covering up an alien encounter. In 1994 an Air Force study concluded it was not a "UFO event" and that no alien ship or alien bodies had been recovered.

Jump to this page **or** follow the pipes.

2012 **Where:** The California State Comptroller's Office in Sacramento, California

Mystery Moolah

The officials who work around here have been hoarding more than $6 billion that doesn't belong to them. No, they're not crooks. The stash is unclaimed money and property from abandoned safe-deposit boxes, checks that couldn't be delivered, unpaid life insurance policies, and so on.

A lot of the stockpile is good old cash, but the officials also hold some rather unusual items—20 pounds of gold bars, a bag stuffed with diamonds, a 1944 issue of ***Our Army*** magazine, and an 86¢ can of Norwegian **sardines** in tomato sauce. Yum!

California isn't alone. State governments across the U.S. are sitting on more than $40 billion worth of stuff that isn't theirs. **New York** leads the way with $12 billion, despite returning $1 million a day to its rightful owners.

Under the law, banks, businesses, and organizations with unclaimed valuables must turn them over to the state they're in. Most states have **websites** people can visit to see if any of that dough is theirs. In the meantime, the money is used to fund govenment operations. The states might also take out ads or set up booths at **state fairs**. Still, it's estimated that 1 in 10 people have unclaimed property they don't know about.

Most payments are a few hundred dollars, but in 2011, one **Missouri** woman raked in a jaw-dropping payday. Her family had invested in a small company years before, then forgotten about it. The state handed her a check for $6.1 million. In 2012 a **Connecticut** man did even better, scoring $32.8 million from the sale of over a million shares of stock he never knew he owned.

I have just one question: "Where do I sign up?"

When does it rain money?
When change is in the air.
Sardine
Where do fish keep their money?
In river banks.
Our Army
Why can't I lend you any money?
Because I'm a little short.

In 2011 lottery tickets worth $800 million were never cashed in.

The government will never send an e-mail about unclaimed money or ask for bank account info. →

iPuzzle

List Price

Time for a little math! Figure out the value of these six unclaimed items, then rank them from 1 (priciest) to 6 (cheapest).

rank: ___ value: $ 250,000

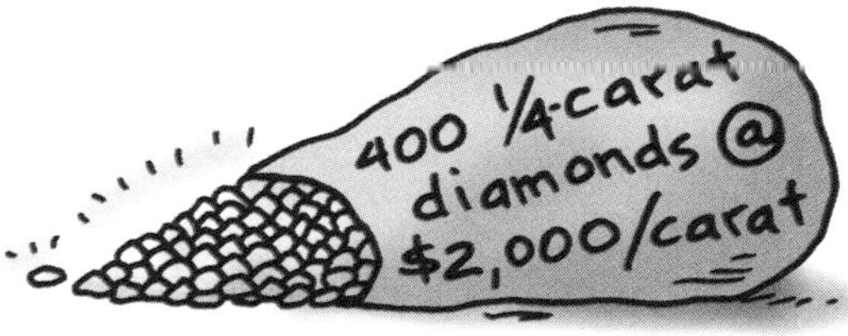

rank: ___ value: $ ______________

rank: ___ value: $ ______________

rank: ___ value: $ ______________

rank: ___ value: $ ______________

rank: ___ value: $ ______________

Mystery Moolah Champs:

U.S. savings bonds account for $16 billion in unclaimed federal money. It's kind of understandable when you realize it can take up to 40 years for the bonds to reach their maximum value. People forget they have them . . . or where they're tucked away.

Jump to this page **or** follow the pipes.

→ Any e-mail (or phone call) that does so is a scam.

2014 **Where:** Off the coast of North Bimini, the Philippines, and Antarctica

Sub Way

Ninety-five percent of the ocean has never been explored, but there's still plenty of weird stuff in the parts we do know about. I had the **S.S. *Throne*** delivered to several spots around the world so I could check out these three oddities....

Squidzilla: Imagine a **squid** as tall as a telephone pole and weighing more than half a ton. It has eyes the size of soccer balls! Such a creature—the **colossal squid**—actually exists, although little is known about it. No one has ever seen one alive in the ocean depths where it lives. Well, no person, that is! I just spotted one here in the **Ross Sea** near **Antarctica** and...okay, I'm getting out of here!

Monster Waves: The **Luzon Strait**, north of the **Philippines**, is home to some of the biggest waves in the world. They can measure the height of a skyscraper! But forget the surfboard because you won't find these waves on the surface. Called **internal waves**, they're made up of colder or saltier water that sweeps across the ocean floor. Understanding internal waves has always been difficult, but scientists are finally starting to unravel how they affect ocean life...and the climate above.

Rocky Road: Near the island of **North Bimini**, a half-mile-long "road" of limestone blocks sits on the ocean bottom, 15 feet down (4.5 meters). The blocks resemble huge bread loaves set side by side, some longer than a person. Dubbed the **Bimini Road**, nobody can agree on whether it's man-made or a natural formation. No cut marks can be seen on the stones, although erosion could have erased any that did exist. A few people have even suggested the road is part of **Atlantis**, a mythical city that sank into the ocean long ago.

In 2014 Tom Peacock and a team of researchers studied internal waves by creating a model.

North Bimini is in the Bahamas, not far from Florida.

iPuzzle

Seascape Escape

Find a path through the seaweed, rock ledges, and sea creatures from START to END.

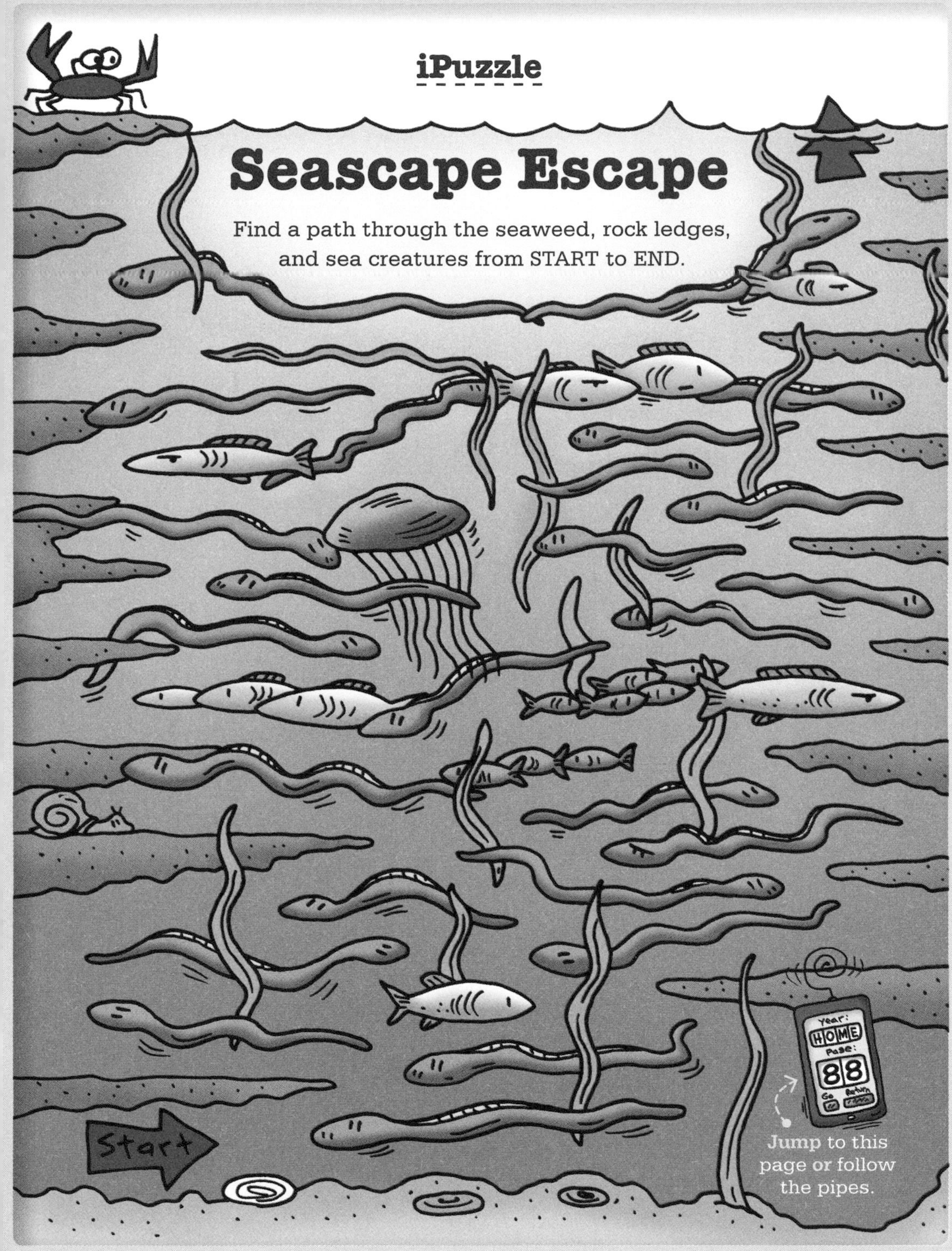

1925

Where: Cuiabá, Brazil, the capital city of the state of Mato Grosso

"Z" End

MILK
MISSING
Have you seen me?
Colonel Percy Fawcett: explorer, mapmaker, archaeologist
MILK

Colonel Percy Fawcett, his son Jack, and a wannabe actor named Raleigh Rimmel have just set out in search of the lost city of **Z**. That's what Fawcett calls an ancient city of fabulous wealth he believes lies hidden in the **Amazon jungle**.

Fawcett, a world-famous archaeologist and explorer, has long suspected Z exists. That belief was reinforced in 1920 after reading **Manuscript 512**, a 1754 Portuguese document in Brazil's **National Library** in **Rio de Janeiro**. Its pages tell of a great city of grand buildings, stone statues, and silver and gold lying on the ground nearby.

How did Fawcett's expedition go? One month into it, he wrote his wife from a place called **Dead Horse Camp**: "You need have no fear of any failure." That was the last anyone ever heard from him!

In 1928 explorer **George Dyott** organized a search for Fawcett. More than 20,000 volunteers answered his ads looking for a crew. He picked four hardy men, added another 21 Brazilian helpers, loaded up 74 oxen and mules, and trudged off in search of Fawcett.

The world feverishly followed Dyott's daily **radio** reports until he had to dump his equipment while fleeing a tribe of angry tribesmen. Months later, Dyott and his crew emerged from the jungle scrawny, ill, and covered in bug bites. They'd failed.

Dyott has picked up Fawcett's trail...

More searches followed—with as many as 100 people losing their lives in the Brazilian jungle. And all anyone ever found were a few small items owned by Fawcett, including a ring he always wore. Had tribesmen, bandits, or hungry jaguars killed Fawcett? Did he die of sickness? Had he been captured? Joined a tribe? The questions are many. The answers…none.

Percy Fawcett was born in Torquay, England, and had the rank of lieutenant colonel in the Royal Artillery.

Jack Fawcett named three of the expedition's mules Dumdum, Gertrude, and Sorehead.

iPuzzle

Fawcett Search

All you have to do in each word-search puzzle is find one name reading left, right, up, down, or diagonally. Sounds easy, but is it?

RALEIGH

H	L	H	R	L	R	A	E
R	I	L	I	A	G	A	R
R	L	E	L	R	L	E	H
A	I	E	H	G	I	R	H
H	G	G	H	A	E	L	L
H	G	I	E	L	A	R	R

PERCY

P	Y	E	P	E	R	P	P
Y	P	R	P	R	P	C	E
P	Y	R	P	C	R	P	P
Y	C	R	E	P	P	E	P
P	R	C	E	Y	Y	P	Y
E	E	Y	P	R	E	P	R

JACK

A	K	A	A	J	C	J	K
K	J	J	A	J	C	A	A
C	C	K	A	K	K	C	C
A	K	K	J	C	A	C	J
A	K	A	J	K	K	K	C
A	J	C	K	C	K	J	A

CHULIM (one of Fawcett's dogs)

M	H	L	C	I	M	M	C
I	C	U	C	H	I	H	H
U	I	H	I	L	L	L	U
C	H	M	C	H	U	I	L
U	U	I	C	M	H	M	C
M	I	U	H	C	C	U	M

Percy Lives: A number of stories and characters have been inspired by Percy Fawcett, including the old man in the animated movie *Up*, an installment of *The Adventures of Tintin*, the Bob Hope movie *Road to Zanzibar*, Sir Arthur Conan Doyle's novel *The Lost World*, and, some think, Indiana Jones. Two movies resulted from George Dyott's search for Fawcett: *Savage Gold* (1933) and *Manhunt in the Jungle* (1958).

Jump to this page **or** follow the pipes.

Peter Fleming, son of Ian Fleming (James Bond's creator), was turned down for George Dyott's mission.

The End

Will wonders never cease—I made it to the end of the book! You did, too, but I knew that was going to be the case. Anyone smart enough to own this book (or even to sneak a peek at someone else's) is certain to speed through it in about six minutes…give or take a month.

Just One Problem

As usual, I've fouled up. I promised on the cover and title page that there would be no limburger in this book. But, cry me a lagoon, just take a look at pages 20, 44, 76, 83, 89, and 94, and you'll find pieces of limburger cheese stinking up the place. Ugh. :-(

But!

To make up for my limburger blunder, please feel free to solve the quiz on the next page at no extra cost!

iPuzzle

Ridiculous Quiz

1. Which of these phrases is an anagram of VOYNICH MANUSCRIPT (the exact same letters rearranged)?
   - **a.** ___ LIMBURGER CHEESE
   - **b.** ___ PLUNGING INTO MYSTERY
   - **c.** ___ PUNY ANCHOR VICTIMS

2. Which of these mothers is NOT mentioned in this book?
   - **a.** ___ Mother Shipton
   - **b.** ___ Leopard Mother
   - **c.** ___ Mother May I

3. Who works in the Oval Office in the White House, and why?
   - **a.** ___ Humpty Dumpty, because he's oval
   - **b.** ___ a racetrack official, because racetracks are oval
   - **c.** ___ the president, because it's his office and it's oval

4. What is a paradox?
   - **a.** ___ a collie and a poodle
   - **b.** ___ two people who have stethoscopes around their necks and ask you to say "ah"
   - **c.** ___ a statement that involves opposite ideas

5. According to an ancient Egyptian dream book, dreaming that you're sitting on top of a palm tree is what?
   - **a.** ___ a sign of good balance
   - **b.** ___ a sign of good climbing skills
   - **c.** ___ a sign of good luck

6. Two children came to Woolpit from a land where the sun never shined. What color were they?
   - **a.** ___ mauve with a hint of puce
   - **b.** ___ plaid
   - **c.** ___ green

Answers

9. Reprint

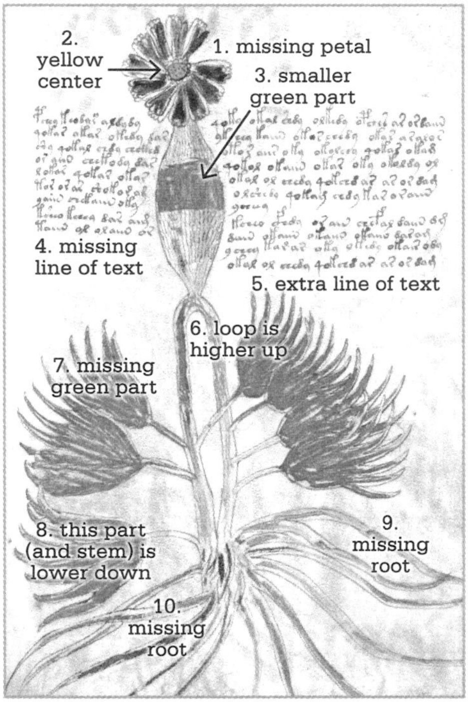

11. Space Race

13. Monster Hunt

N	T	S	A	E	B	X	Z	O	U	C	S
O	E	B	L	S	M	O	T	N	A	H	P
M	T	F	L	O	W	E	R	E	W	W	O
E	U	O	I	O	I	J	Q	R	L	A	L
D	R	K	Z	V	B	M	V	I	Q	O	C
N	B	I	G	F	O	O	T	P	T	R	Y
E	R	G	O	T	J	C	A	M	E	G	C
I	I	C	H	U	P	A	C	A	B	R	A
F	E	G	G	I	A	N	T	V	I	L	I
U	T	F	Y	M	M	U	M	V	A	U	P
W	E	O	I	M	R	F	S	U	Q	R	K
D	L	W	V	E	I	B	M	O	Z	N	I

15. Wat•erg•ate

1. NEWSCAST
2. EARPLUG
3. WAIST
4. PANTHER
5. ICEBERG
6. AFTER
7. MATTRESS
8. ENERGY
9. SWEATY
10. CASTLE
11. AVERAGE
12. BREATHE
13. STARTLE
14. WALLET
15. WREATH
16. ROWBOAT
17. UNDERDOG
18. CHAPTER
19. EMERGE
20. CANTEEN

17. Which Witch?

Number 5 is identical to the original.

1: eye closed
2: cane handle
3: right hand is moved down
4: end of yellow scarf
6: nose
7: end of hat

19. Sea-doku

1. 2. 3.

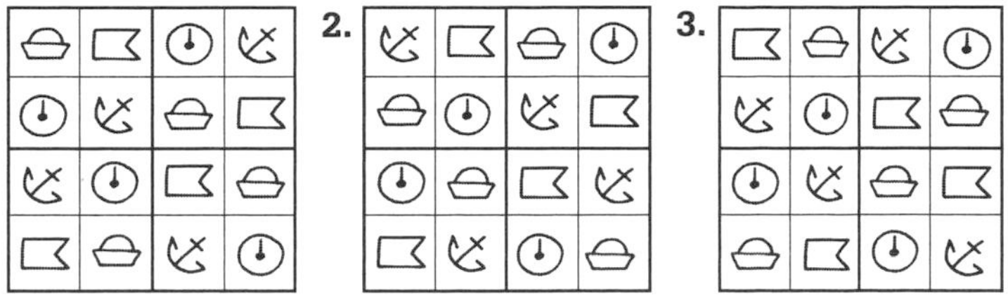

23. Label Maker

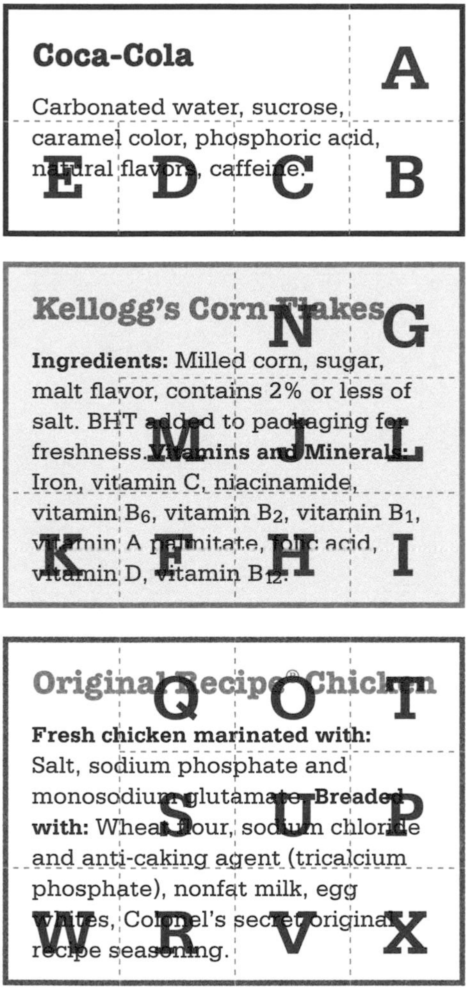
Coca-Cola
Carbonated water, sucrose, caramel color, phosphoric acid, natural flavors, caffeine.
A
E D C B
Kellogg's Corn Flakes
N G
Ingredients: Milled corn, sugar, malt flavor, contains 2% or less of salt. BHT added to packaging for freshness. Vitamins and Minerals: Iron, vitamin C, niacinamide, vitamin B6, vitamin B2, vitamin B1, vitamin A palmitate, folic acid, vitamin D, vitamin B12.
M J L
K F H I
Original Recipe® Chicken
Q O T
Fresh chicken marinated with: Salt, sodium phosphate and monosodium glutamate. Breaded with: Wheat flour, sodium chloride and anti-caking agent (tricalcium phosphate), nonfat milk, egg whites, Colonel's secret original recipe seasoning.
S U P
W R V X

25. Bird Watching

1-C 2-I 3-H 4-D 5-B 6-A 7-F 8-G 9-E

27. The Prez

Deacon: Carter
Eagle: Clinton
Passkey: Ford
Rawhide: Reagan
Renegade: Obama
Searchlight: Nixon
Timberwolf: H.W. Bush
Tumbler: W. Bush

29. The Rock

FORTY FEET BELOW TWO MILLION POUNDS ARE BURIED

31. Paradox

A-6 B-8 C-9 D-10 E-1
F-3 G-7 H-2 I-4 J-5

33. May I Cut In?

Pieces 3 and 5 don't match exactly.

35. Tarzan of the Apes

2. NAZRAT
3. NAZR
4. NAZRES
5. NAMRES
6. SERMAN
7. SUPERMAN ⟵ *Born on Krypton, he was raised by humans on Earth.*

2. TALAN
3. ALAN
4. NALA
5. KALA

37. Missing Bomb

1. FOAM RUBBER
2. BLABBERMOUTH
3. PLUMB BOB
4. BAMBOO
5. BOOKMOBILE
6. BELL-BOTTOMS
7. MOBBED
8. MUMBO JUMBO
9. IMPROBABLE
10. MOTHER HUBBARD

Extra credit:

11. BABY BOOMER

39. Canoe Find It?

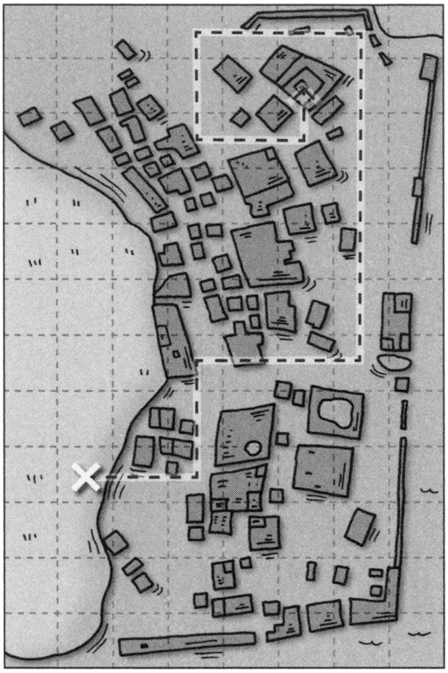

41. Oops!

2-H WOODPECKER
3-I NONSTOP
4-A SNOOPY
5-J POOPER SCOOPER
6-E MICROSCOPE
7-D HULA-HOOP
8-F MONOPOLY
9-B LOLLIPOP
10-C TOOTHPICK

Extra-extra credit: PHILOSOPHY

45. Good or Bad?

1. 11 = GOOD
2. 5 = BAD
3. 7 = BAD
4. 11 = GOOD
5. 8 = BAD
6. 9 = BAD
7. 12 = GOOD
8. 12 = GOOD
9. 12 = GOOD
10. 13 = GOOD
11. 8 = BAD

47-48. Concert-tration

1. three people
2. one person standing
3. two paintings
4. black and white tiles
5. a stringed instrument
6. light coming from the left
7. none of them
8. forward

51. Look! Up in the Sky!

EXPERIMENTAL PLANE
WEATHER BALLOON
EMERGENCY FLARE
MILITARY AIRCRAFT
SATELLITE THE MOON
CLOUD FORMATIONS
METEOR FIREBALL
FLOCK OF BIRDS

53. Pipe Up

55. Spy Jokes

1. COUNTER SPIES
2. PLANTS AND BUGS
3. UNDERCOVER AGENTS
4. S, P, E, and L

57. Whodunit?

The woman in the bottom row to the right of the cat. (It's Phyllis Tanks.)

59. Like Clockwork

1. LUNA-TICK 2. IT WAS BRIGHTER

61. Greenery

2. I HO**PE A** GREEN…
3. …HIM A S**LIM E**DGE.
4. ATTILA THE **HUN TER**RIFIED…
5. THE ESKI**MOS S**AILED…
6. WE OF**FER N**O…
7. …SILVER NIC**KEL LY**ING…
8. HE TOOK A VITA**MIN T**ABLET…
9. …HI**S HAM, ROCK**ED!
10. …**FOR EST**IMATING…

iPuzzle Quickie: 1. B 2. C 3. A

63. How Puzzling

1. The correct route spells THERE IS NO POSSIBLE WAY

2. 25 + 6 + 19 = 50

65. Rat Latin

WELCOME TO THE CLUB.
DO YOU LIKE LIMBURGER?

ATI LATIKE YATOUR TATAIL.
DWATAYNE ATIS TATHE BATEST.
CATOULD YATOU SQATUEAK ATUP?
ATI LATIVE ATON ATA FATARM.

Extra credit: 2. BATH MAT
3. MEAT & POTATOES
4. WEATHER STATION

67. Whinny Ha Ha

1. G 2. B 3. D 4. J 5. H
6. A 7. I 8. F 9. C 10. E

69. Stone Work

71. Something's Different

1. bigger nose
2. smaller chin
3. mean eyebrows
4. elf ear
5. mouth lowered
6. eyeball position
7. longer hair bun
8. smile
9. bigger forehead
10. shoulders

73. What's Dot?

It's Dwayne!

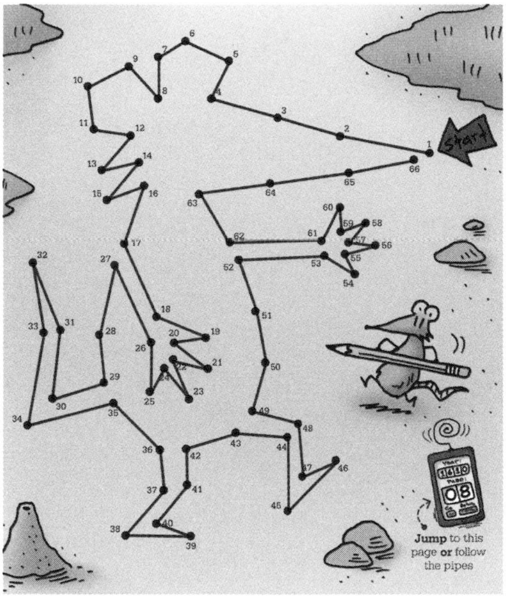

75. Buried Letters

A CHEST PROTECTOR

79. Hop to It

81. UFOdoku

1.

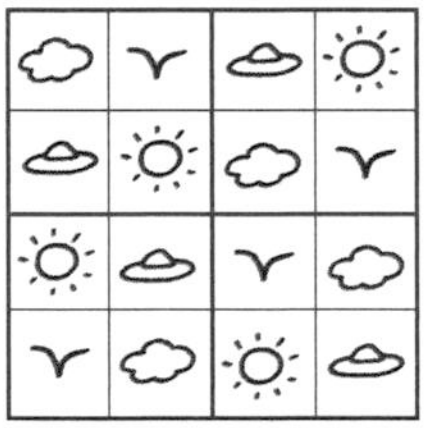

2.

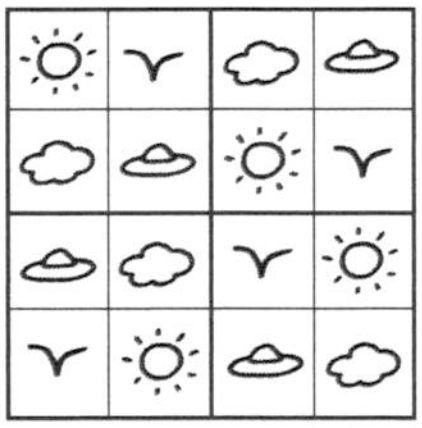

3.

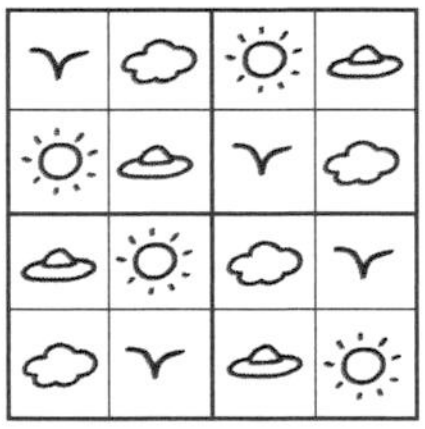

83. List Price

1. sardines
   500,000 x .86 = $430,000
2. gold bars
   20 × 1,200 × 16 = $384,000
3. topaz
   3,000 x 100 = $300,000
4. silver coins = $250,000
5. diamonds
   400 x .25 (1/4) x 2,000 = $200,000
6. limburger
   10,000 x 15 = $150,000

85. Seascape Escape

87. Fawcett Search

H L H R L R A E
R I L I A G A R
R L E L R L E H
A I E H G I R H
H G G H A E L L
(H G I E L A R) R

P Y E P E R P P
Y P R P R P C E
P Y R P C R P P
(Y C R E P) P E P
P R C E Y Y P Y
E E Y P R E P R

A K A A J C J K
K J J A J C A A
C C K A K K C C
A K K J C A C J
A K A J K K K C
A J C K C K J A

M H L C I M M C
I C U C H I H H
U I H I L L L U
C H M C H U I L
U U I C M H M C
M I U H C C U M

89. Ridiculous Quiz

The correct answer for each question is "c."

Do You Own the Other iFlush books?

Swimming in Science

Hurtling thru History

Hunting for Heroes

Other outrageously cool **For Kids Only!** titles:

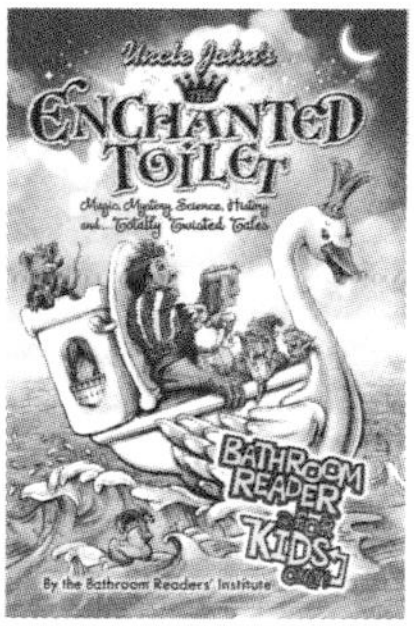

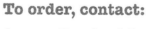

To order, contact:

Bathroom Readers' Press
P.O. Box 1117
Ashland, OR 97520
Phone: 888-488-4642
Fax: 541-482-6159

www.bathroomreader.com

iBonus

Create a Mystery Hunt

What you'll need: a few sheets of graph paper, a pencil, a photocopier, and a prize (perhaps a trophy you mold out of aluminum foil and/or a first-place certificate).

How it works:

1. You'll hand each contestant a word search you've created.

2. When a contestant solves the word search, you'll hand them directions to *find* a maze you've created.

3. When a contestant solves the maze, you'll hand them a hint for finding the prize.

4. The first person to find the prize, gets to keep it!

Make your puzzles:

Word Search

1. Make a list of words that fit a theme. For example, pizza toppings or zoo animals.

2. Take a sheet of graph paper and draw a line around a box that's 12 squares across and 12 squares down.

3. Write as many of the words in the 12 x 12 box as you can. Mix it up so they read left, right, up, down, and diagonally. If some cross, all the better!

4. Once the words are in place, fill the blank squares with random letters.

5. Write the list of hidden words in alphabetical order below your puzzle.

Maze

1. Draw a large rectangular box on a sheet of graph paper.

2. Write START in the upper left. Write END in the lower right.

3. Plot out a twisting route from START to END. Use the graph paper lines as guides for the walls.

4. Add in some wrong turns along the way, each leading to a dead end.

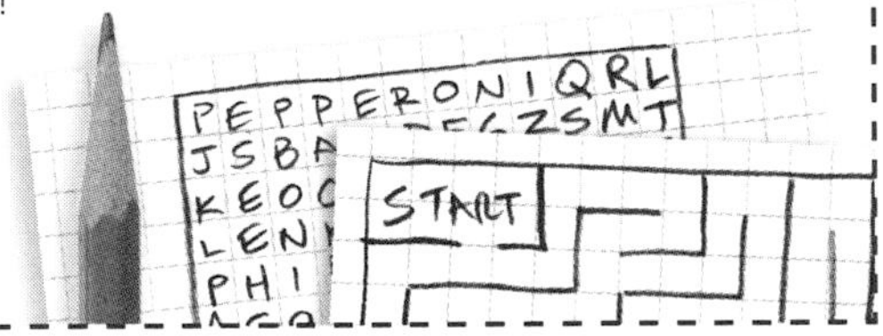

Finish:

1. Pick a hiding spot for the mazes. Write ***clear directions*** to that location on a sheet of paper.

2. Hide the prize. Write a ***hint*** that will help in finding the prize without saying exactly where it is. For example, you might say, "It's under a soft place where you'd sleep" (which could be a bed or a sofa).

3. Photocopy enough puzzles, directions, and hints for all of your contestants.

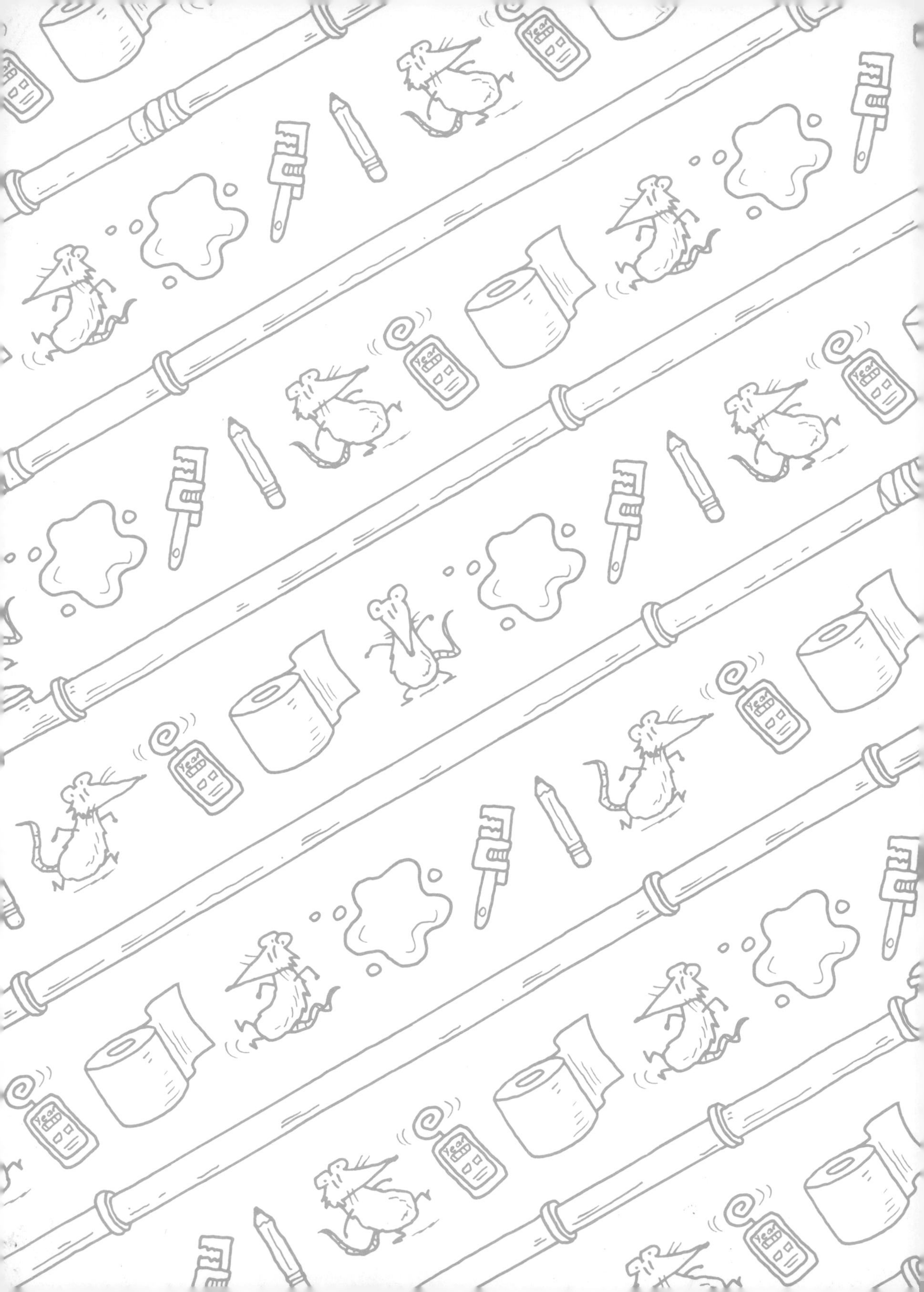